WRESTLING WITH ANGELS

Other books by this author:

Well-driven Nails
Out of the Pit: Joseph's Story and Yours
Behind the Seen: God's Hand in Esther's Life . . . and Yours

To order, call 1-800-765-6955.

To order additional copies of *Wrestling With Angels,* by Larry L. Lichtenwalter, call 1-800-765-6955.

LARRY L. LICHTENWALTER

WRESTLING WITH ANGELS

In the Grip of Jacob's God

REVIEW AND HERALD® PUBLISHING ASSOCIATION
HAGERSTOWN, MD 21740

The author assumes full responsibility for the accuracy of all facts and quotations as cited in this book.

This book was
Edited by Gerald Wheeler
Copyedited by Lori Halvorsen and James Cavil
Designed by Emily Harding/Mark O'Connor
Interior by Toya Koch
Typeset: 12/14 Bembo

PRINTED IN U.S.A.

06 05 04 03 02   5 4 3 2 1

R&H Cataloging Service
Lichtenwalter, Larry Lee, 1952–
    Wrestling with angels: In the grip of Jacob's God.

    1. Jacob (Biblical patriarch).   I. Title.
            220.92

ISBN 0-8280-1623-2

DEDICATION

To Dad and Mom,
Linda, Lisa, and Lynn . . .
We've done our share of wrestling.
We've experienced incredible dysfunction.
But we're still family!
No matter what we've been through together,
the God who has healed us along the way
still promises our family a blessing.

CONTENTS

MIRACLE ON THE MAT

Alexander Karelin hadn't lost a wrestling match in 13 years. The monstrous 286-pound Russian Greco-Roman wrestler hadn't even given up so much as a single point in 10 years of international competition. An Olympic champion, he had claimed the gold three times. He proved so intimidating that on two occasions at the Barcelona games his opponent rolled over and pinned himself instead of letting himself be pulped by the great Russian. Karelin had a knack for throwing his opponent off balance. He was known, though, for his signature move—the Karelin Lift—in which through sheer strength he would literally pick up a nearly 300-pound opponent, twist him around, and slam him down. But the three-time Olympic champion was upset by a relatively unknown jumbo Wyoming farm boy named Rulon Gardner.

My sons told me about the surprise upset one afternoon during the 2000 Sydney Olympics. "Dad," my oldest said excitedly, "last night some farm boy from Wyoming defeated a famous Russian wrestling champ. We need to watch it."

For a moment I remembered the hours I had spent with my dad watching professional wrestling aired from New York's Madison Square Garden—something I hadn't done since a teenager. "Why not? It's the Olympics. It's a great story." And what a match! During the entire encounter Karelin kept trying to take his usual control of the situation, seeking to use his celebrated Karelin Lift. The Russian attempted to intimidate Gardner, throw him off balance, or wear him down. All the 29-year-old Gardner would do was press his hulking body up against Karelin's. As a result Karelin kept having to back up or reposition himself so he could establish an offensive position again. Gardner was so persistent that Karelin literally spent his energy trying to keep his opponent's body at bay. As the minutes passed, the Russian athlete became noticeably exhausted. With five seconds left in overtime a wearied Karelin shocked the crowd by dropping his hands, surrendering the match, and stepping away, defeated. The Wyoming farm boy who could carry four 100-pound bales of hay at a time (two in each hand) was too much for him. Gardner had worn him down.[1]

It reminds me of another wrestling match in which an undefeated wrestler found himself outmatched, utterly exhausted, and ready to throw in the towel. In fact he clung to his powerful opponent, and begged for mercy. "During the night Jacob got up and sent his two wives, two concubines, and eleven sons across the Jabbok River. After they were on the other side, he sent over all his possessions. This left Jacob all alone in the camp, and a man came and wrestled with him until dawn. When the man saw that he couldn't win the match, he struck Jacob's hip and knocked it out of joint at the socket. Then the man said, 'Let me go, for it is dawn.' But Jacob panted, 'I will not let you go unless you bless me.' 'What is your name?' the man asked. He replied, 'Jacob.' 'Your name will no longer be Jacob,' the man told him. 'It is now Israel, because you have struggled with both God and men and have won.' 'What is your name?' Jacob asked him. 'Why do you ask?' the man replied. Then he blessed Jacob there. Jacob named the place Peniel—'face of God'—for he said, 'I have seen God face to face, yet my life has been spared.' The sun rose as he left Peniel, and he was limping because of his hip" (Gen. 32:22-31, NLT).

Jacob was a fighter. He was a person who would never suffer defeat at the hands of anyone or anything, whether it was his hotheaded brother Esau, his conniving uncle Laban, his quarreling wives, his worldly-wise children, even God. The patriarch was clever, strong, resourceful, capable, resilient, scheming—in a word, competitive. He was undefeated. But on this night Jacob met his match and finally capitulated.[2]

It was a marathon of nightlong wrestling in pitch darkness with an antagonist he couldn't see. Alone on the shores of the Jabbok River, Jacob was nearing the end of his homeward journey with the prospect of meeting up with Esau. He wouldn't learn his estranged brother's attitude toward him until morning. But this night, on the eve of that fateful reckoning, Jacob took stock of where he had been and what he had become. The patriarch found himself forced to face the spirits that haunted him, to work out his forebodings about his own failures, and to weigh what he had to do the next day. He must either reconcile with his brother or find a way to escape their confrontation with his life.[3] Thus Jewish philosopher Martin Buber sees "Jacob's wrestling as a metaphor for all of humanity's struggling with life's existential questions."[4] "Jacob's nocturnal wrestling with his unknown, unnamed antagonist," Buber writes, "is understood by the ancient Jewish interpreters . . . as the decisive encounter between Jacob and the divine advocate of Esau. This reading is indeed the only reading that makes sense of the struggle in the place where it is recounted, i.e., between Jacob's apprehension over the ensuing encounter with the brother he once so maliciously betrayed and the auspicious outcome of that encounter."[5] Jacob's wrestling with God was thus linked to all that was going on deep inside him before he encountered Esau. His wrestling with God was linked, too, to all that went on inside him that next morning as he anxiously sought reconciliation with Esau.

This inner struggle is clearly conveyed in the biblical account of the conclusion of Jacob's night of wrestling. Jacob named this place of intense struggle "Peniel—'face of God'—for he said, 'I have seen God face to face, yet my life has been spared'" (verse 30, NLT). Earlier that day the patriarch had anxiously said to himself, "I will wipe the anger from Esau's face with the gift that goes ahead of my face; afterward, when I see his face, perhaps he will lift up my face!" (verse 20, paraphrase). Later this same apprehension echoed in the auspicious resolution he experienced with Esau: "For I have, after all, seen your face, as one sees the face of God, and you have been gracious to me" (Gen. 33:10, paraphrase). Jacob meets the entire experience with apprehension about himself, about Esau—as well as God. He wrestles through the night with God, but Esau and his own self are fully in view. He had good reason to wonder if reconciliation was possible with the brother he hadn't seen for 20 years, the brother from whom he had stolen the birthright, the brother who was rapidly approaching with a band of 400 warriors. Jacob had good reason to fear what might happen. His midnight encounter with an unknown assailant belonged to and formed part of the struggle he anticipated with Esau. Without doubt, whoever the unknown wrestler was, he at least partially represented Esau.[6] Jacob was wrestling with God, but it was with Esau on his mind and all his family and personal failures haunting him that the battle took place. The patriarch was struggling with himself—and God—in the setting of the moral/spiritual effect of family failure and dysfunction. By morning he is reconciled with God, but he also comes to terms with his brother and himself. Before it is all over, Jacob experiences a new sense of identity, new spiritual/moral power, a new name, and a new relationship with both God and his brother. He no longer wrestles.

His night of wrestling is a metaphor for all our struggles with life's questions. And that existential wrestling sits squarely in the context of family—particularly, dysfunctional family. Family is where our identity and sense of self is formed. It is where we become who we are, as the values and choices and personalities (and the dysfunction) expressed in our household shape us. Family forms those inner points of reference about ourselves and others that—whether right or wrong—we find hard to veer from. Even when they destroy us.

The family is where we learn to win or lose, where we are shamed or favored. Within the framework of family we learn grace by being graced or we experience ungrace as we are treated roughly, unfairly, without compassion. Family embodies both our limitless capacity for love and competition as well as that of betrayal and forgiveness.[7] According to Buber, "all actual life is encounter"[8]—encounter with others, that is. And the most significant part of actual life is encounter with family. That's where we experience the greatest pain, ask the deepest questions about who we are, and make the most critical choices that not only shape our own character but our family's character and culture as well. It is in our encounter with family that we instinctively look for meaning, love, belonging, and enduring existence. Our family is where we first look to satisfy our hunger for a spiritual identity and a system of values to guide our lives.

Not surprisingly, family is where every one of us fundamentally encounters God.

The Jacob narrative is the story of family. It is an epic account with vivid characters in dramatic circumstances, a virtual multigenerational saga of the all-too-human struggle of faith and faithfulness, relating and relationships. Here we find the seemingly incidental experiences of private individuals, of parent, spouse, sibling, and child. The narrative also portrays incredible dysfunction. Perhaps there is no biblical family more unhealthy, more out of sorts than Jacob's. His family's tale of unhappy relationships and intense personal pain carries a profound message for all hurting families. These tales from the household of Jacob talk about spiritual identity, personal accountability, interpersonal relationships, and individual moral purpose. Genesis records the longing and lifelong search for a blessing. In these biblical experiences we find played out sibling rivalry, parental power struggles, and the alienation that flows from dysfunctional behavior. They reveal the consequences of choices, the impact of envy, greed, and hopefully, reconciliation. The story of his family shows how contemporary culture still challenges family health and underlines the critical need of building a Christian family culture. Jacob's experiences demonstrate the pain of loss and grief and the destructive patterns that often follow. His family reveals what every family needs to leave the next generation. In Genesis we find mirrored our own families. Perhaps you will meet yourself in Jacob as you find painful similarities between his family and yours. I trust you will discover hope and perspective as well.

Again, Jacob's night of wrestling is a metaphor for all our struggles with life's questions. And more than we realize, that existential wrestling sits squarely in the context of family.

So who is the "man" who wrestles with Jacob on the riverbank and finally blesses him with a new name? "God," we say.[9] Scripture says as much, and that's how Jacob saw it. Referring to this moment in Jacob's life, Hosea wrote: "Before Jacob was born, he struggled with his brother; when he became a man, he even fought with God. Yes, he wrestled with the angel and won. He wept and pleaded for a blessing from him" (Hosea 12:3, 4, NLT). Jacob "fought with God." He "wrestled with the angel." Which is it? Through the centuries artists have developed the picture of Jacob wrestling with the angel in their etchings, reliefs, tapestries, or paintings. The imagery of "wrestling with angels" is a theme that runs through the entire account of Jacob and his family.[10] In reality, Jacob wrestles with many angels, predominately the Angel of the Lord Himself. Paul's words to the Ephesians allude to such wide-ranging struggles: "For we do not wrestle against flesh and blood, but against principalities, against powers, against the rulers of the darkness of this age, against spiritual hosts of wickedness in the heavenly *places*" (Eph. 6:12, NKJV). Here Paul refers not only to demonic forces, but to the very structures and systems of evil. Evidently, he sees not only the demonic beings themselves but also the world of ideas, values, and attitudes that they embody and the responses they engender in our lives. It includes the people of the world—other human beings through whom the spiritual powers work against us—as well. That is the nature of all the angels we wrestle.

Ultimately, Jacob is the story of the conquest of self. Our greatest personal problem is our self. It is not circumstances, disabilities, enemies, or even family, but what lies within.[11] Through the life of Jacob God preaches a "gospel of recovery."[12] It proclaims recovery not just for individuals, but for families. As Sanders writes, "The God of Jacob is preeminently the God of the second chance to the Christian who has failed and failed persistently. The second—or twenty-second—chance does not necessarily avert the temporal consequences of past failure, but even that failure can be a stepping-stone to new victories. . . . The supreme lesson of Jacob's story is that no failure need be final. There is hope with the God of Jacob for any temperament, any disposition. No past failure puts the possibility out of reach. When God has saved and apprehended a man, He pursues him with undiscourageable perseverance with the sole purpose of blessing him."[13] Such hope of God's gracious pursuit and upset includes families—your family.

Interestingly, with God, when we lose, we win. Hosea tells us Jacob beat God. In spite of the limp and the surrender, he won! When Jacob surrendered and God *threw* him, he won. Jacob took the gold because God took the heart. Whenever we give in to the grip of Jacob's God we too, will win.

One more thought before we step into the colorful life of Jacob and his family. As Madeleine L' Engle observes, "Jacob's angel wrestled with him all night. We don't always have the courage to keep it up as long as that, though night is often a time for the most intense spiritual struggle, and we don't always know who started it—we, with our unanswerable questions, or the angel, leaping on us unexpectedly. Perhaps we need the angel to start grappling with us, to turn us aside from the questions which have easy answers to those which cause us to grow, no matter how painful that growth can be."[14] Hopefully *Wrestling With Angels* will be part of God's intended growth for you. May it turn you toward the kind of intensely personal issues and questions that will cause you to grow, no matter how painful that growth might be, and in the process, may you find the living God whose only desire is to bless. When through life's inner struggles and painful turns you find yourself in the grip of Jacob's God, may you too no longer wrestle.

---

[1] Joel Stein, "Rulon Gardner: A Jumbo Wyoming Farm Boy Shocks the World, and Himself, by Wrangling a Russian Tank," *Time*, Oct. 9, 2000, p. 100.

[2] J. Oswald Sanders, *Spiritual Manpower* (Chicago: Moody Press, 1965), p. 31.

[3] Bill Moyers, *Genesis: A Living Conversation* (New York: Doubleday, 1996), pp. 296, 297.

[4] Naomi H. Rosenblatt and Joshua Horwitz, *Wrestling With Angels: What the First Family of Genesis Teaches Us About Our Spiritual Identity, Sexuality, and Personal Relationships* (New York: Delacorte Press, 1995), pp. 298, 299.

[5] Martin Buber & Franz Rosenzweig, *Scripture and Translation* (Bloomington, Ind.: Indiana University Press, 1994), p. 137. Buber further writes: "Moreover, it is only this interpretation that permits us to see into, or up toward, the reasons for this course of events, reasons which even then defy our understanding but at least command our respect. We may feel, of course, that the ancient interpretation reads something into the text that is not there, perhaps as a rationalization. But this can be shown not to be the case, precisely from the linking of the nocturnal struggle both to the apprehension that precedes and the solution that follows it" *(ibid.)*.

[6] Moyers, pp. 296, 297.

[7] Rosenblatt and Horwitz, p. xiii.

[8] Martin Buber, *I and Thou* (New York: Charles Scribner's Sons, 1970), p. 62.

[9] "His [God's] character finds even more direct expression when he first tells the son [Jacob] of that son [Isaac] to return from Aram to Canaan, and thereafter attacks him or causes him to be attacked and dislocates his hip while wrestling. At this point the tradition is not yet fully interested in ascribing everything to YHVH himself, and so the one who performs the action is 'a man,' but that God stands behind cannot be doubted. Unlike the narrative of the attack on Moses, the motif of the 'dread night,' which is merely hinted at here, is expanded in repeated keywords. By the nocturnal struggle with the divine being, by holding the 'man' fast until a blessing is obtained, Jacob passes the test. His leading God had ordered him to wander, the same God who had once promised him: 'See, I am with you, I shall protect you wherever you go, and shall bring you back to this land.' And now that he had returned to this land, the wanderer had to face the perilous encounter before he enjoyed the final grace of God" (Martin Buber, *Moses: The Revelation and the Covenant*

[New York: Harper & Brothers, Publishers, 1946], pp. 57, 58).

[10] I've gleaned the imagery "wrestling with angels" and many helpful insights from Naomi H. Rosenblatt and Joshua Horwitz's book on Genesis, *Wrestling With Angels*. But while adopting the metaphor, I have taken a decidedly different—and what I consider more biblical—track in presenting the stories of this biblical first family. Although sensitive to the sociological and psychological nuances they elicit from the story, my focus is more toward the concrete and objective moral and spiritual aspects the story brings to life. I read Genesis as inspired story and commentary, as something far more than legend and tales. We do not find the solutions to our existential wrestlings in psychology or the humanistic dynamics of existentialism, but in the living God and the values and principles of life and relationships that He conveys through such biblical stories as these.

[11] Roy L. Laurin, *Designed for Conquest* (Grand Rapids: Kregel Publications, 1990), p. 20.

[12] Sanders, p. 36.

[13] *Ibid.*

[14] *Ibid.*

HAIRY HUNTER AND SHAVEN CHEF

one

(Genesis 25:21-34)

WHO WOULD THINK of putting Arnold Schwarzenegger and Danny DeVito together and calling them twins? It takes a zany imagination and a strong sense of humor to place them in the same family. They're opposites in size, appearance, and the kind of character they usually personify in the movies they star in. And twins? Come on! But that's just what Hollywood wanted to caricature in its wacky tale called *Twins* in which a top-secret genetic experiment produces two baby boys rather than one. Although separated at birth, they finally find each other at age 35. Schwarzenegger plays Julius, who turns out to be a perfect specimen of a man both in body and soul. Strong, polite, kind, and innocent, he is honest to the core. DeVito depicts Vincent, who turns out to be a lecherous petty criminal, a real creep. But they are brothers. Twins. And once together, they go look-ing for Mom. Absurd contrasts, they are a comical pair and a juxtapo-sition of values.

For that matter, who would think of lumping Jacob and Esau together and calling them twins? The hairy hunter and the shaven chef? The macho man and the mama's boy? The rough-and-tumble adventuresome son and the granola-eating homebody? But their story is no Hollywood comedy, no zany caricaturing of life. Real family, they were an agonizing portrayal of stark contrasts, resentful competition, and painful collision.

The story of Jacob is a vivid story of spirited self and a bitter struggle for personal survival. He competed with his brother for the perceived blessing—from Mom and Pop and God!

It all began in the "war womb." When Rebekah finally became pregnant after years of infertility, she felt herself wracked by pain, as if her womb had become an unrelenting and vicious battleground. "The children struggled together within her," Scripture tells us, making her so miserable that she cried out to God, "Why do I exist? What does this mean?" (Gen. 25:22). They kicked and wrestled in the watery darkness, two bodies feeding off one placenta, fighting for nourishment and—most of all—for space apart from the other. Anyone who's ever seen a sonogram of prenatal twins can appreciate just how physically Jacob and Esau competed for nurture and room in their mother's womb. There never seems to be enough space.

One can only wonder about the psychological impact such in utero closeness engenders. The Hebrew word translated struggled means "to crush, get crushed, be broken in pieces, to oppress, or be oppressed." The book of Judges uses it to describe a woman dropping a millstone down on Abimelech's head from the tower he was attacking, smashing his skull (Judges 9:53), and in Deuteronomy God warns Israel that in the event of their apostasy, "a people whom you do not know shall eat up the produce of your ground and all your labors, and you shall never be anything but oppressed and crushed continually. You shall be driven mad by the sight of what you see" (Deut. 28:33, 34, NASB). Being squeezed out or crushed by someone else is never a comfortable experience for any of us. When it continues endlessly, it can drive us insane. We instinctively protect self by fighting back— wrestling. No wonder Jacob came out of the womb "grasping Esau's heel" (Gen. 25:26, NIV)—"symbolic of the power struggle that would characterize his lifelong relationship with his brother."[1]

Samuel Alexander Armas' parents love to show off photos of their baby boy, particularly one taken nearly four months before his birth. The photo, shot during in utero surgery to correct a birth defect, depicts Samuel's penny-sized fist reaching outside Julie Armas' womb, grasping at a doctor's finger. Samuel was the youngest fetus to have surgery. Doctors opened his mother's womb August 19,

1999, and closed the gap in his spine caused by spina bifida, a congenital disease that often leads to paralysis and other problems. As Dr. Joseph Bruner prepared to close the womb, Samuel thrust his fist through the surgical opening. Gently Bruner tucked the tiny hand back inside and finished the procedure, but not before freelance photographer Michael Clancy captured the stunning moment.

The tiny fist has added fuel to an international abortion debate, appearing on anti-abortion billboards in Ireland and in newspapers in France, Germany, Norway, Singapore, and the United States. Abortion opponents say the image shows that fetuses—even at only 21 weeks—are viable and aware.[2] This is more than fetal tissue! Scientific studies of unborn children are demonstrating more and more that brain activity begins early after conception takes place. God's comment on the struggle taking place between Jacob and Esau has tremendous implications regarding human life existing in the womb: "There are two nations in your womb, your issue will be two rival peoples. One nation will have the mastery of the other, and the elder will serve the younger" (verse 23, New Jerusalem). As they pressed hard against each other in Rebekah's womb, God knew where it would all lead and even how the in utero crushing would frame their life perspectives.[3] "Though supernatural events were definitely involved in this prenatal activity, God still used natural capacities in these unborn babies to cause this communication to take place."[4]

Jacob and Esau's crushing embrace in the womb was only the beginning of their decades-long struggle for supremacy. It offered a preview of the way they would behave toward each other for the better part of their lives and pointed to what lay ahead for themselves, for their family, and for the larger society. Theirs is "the story of a generation born in conflict,"[5] illustrating that no level of social organization is immune from conflict and division, domination and subordination. "Conflict at one level in a society affects all other levels."[6] The rivalry between Jacob and Esau eventually shaped almost all possible relationships. It extended to their parents and reached beyond their immediate family to touch both distant relatives and next-door neighbors. The rivalry even marked their relationship with God.[7]

Thus sibling rivalry and family conflict becomes a central theme throughout the last half of Genesis. "The story has almost no times of rest and quiet. The family is either in conflict or on the move, and often the two dynamics overlap."[8] Such discord disturbed even sleep, leading to the terror of attack during a night at the Jabbok riverbank. The next generation—Jacob's sons—would learn the lessons well and push their rivalry to the point of nearly destroying the family altogether.

Here Scripture brings us face to face with the social realm of families—that what happens between siblings takes place in the family, and what occurs in the family plays itself out in society. "The family is a microcosm for the larger world, the first place where we learn to compete for the things we need"[9]—including the family of God! The same kinds of issues we deal with personally in the home often flow over into our interpersonal relationships within the church. Family is the place where we develop social skills and where we come to grips with our own personal ethics as well as the integrity and patterns of our own interpersonal relationships. Self and struggle in the family is where we often come to grips with where God really is in our own lives. Everyone of us is part of a family, whether as brother or sister, a son or daughter, mother or father, uncle or aunt, cousin, grandparent, or even brother or sister in the faith.

Jacob longed to escape his personal pain, moral confusion, and spiritual emptiness. He needed a way out of his family's dysfunction and codependency. Somehow he must overcome his confrontational, competitive, and self-protecting spirit. Every member of his family had that same need, although with differing intensity depending on each person's personality and the point at issue. Such spiritual wrestling lasted for generations.

As we study Jacob's story, hopefully we'll see the way through the darkness of dysfunction that just may haunt some of our own relationships.

INGREDIENTS FOR FAMILY FAILURE

Right now I want us to notice some of the basic ingredients for family failure and interpersonal conflict that the Jacob narrative presents.

First, Jacob and Esau had radically different personalities. They were worlds apart in their likes and dislikes, opposites in disposition and character, and at odds in how they viewed life. "When the boys grew up, Esau became a skillful hunter, a man of the field, but Jacob was a peaceful man, living in tents" (verse 27, NASB).

Esau was the macho outdoors type—athletic, adventuresome, a man of action, impulsive. He would get caught up in the moment and in his physical needs. The staccato-like action words at the end of Genesis 25 capture his personality and outlook—he ate, drank, rose up, left, and spurned his birthright (verse 34). His response to Jacob indicates an emotional guy prone to exaggerate things. First he announces, "I am famished." Then he declares, "I am about to die" (verses 30, 32, NASB).

Patriarchs and Prophets tells us that "Esau grew up loving self-gratification and centering all his interests in the present. Impatient of restraint, he delighted in the wild freedom of the chase, and early chose the life of a hunter."[10]

In comparison Jacob seems bland, almost boring. In fact, Scripture portrays Jacob as a quiet sort who preferred to stay inside his tent (verse 27). Up in his room, so to speak. A domesticated homebody, he was a soft-hands gourmet cook sheltered from and naive about life. Jacob was definitely introverted, with little noticeable vision, ambition, or energy. I can see him at the stove sautéing onions and garlic, simmering tomatoes and lentils, or baking bread. Today we might call him a granola-eating yuppie.

Yet Jacob was by no means innocent or harmless. Calculating, determined, and shrewd, he knew what he wanted. He was someone who traded the momentary for the long-range.

An almost unbridgeable chasm loomed between these two brothers' respective cultures, personalities, temperaments. They were brothers—twins, no less—going in entirely different directions.

Second, Jacob and Esau experienced lopsided relationships with their parents. Parental favoritism is transparent in this story. "Now Isaac loved Esau, because he had a taste for game, but Rebekah loved Jacob" (verse 28, NASB). As parents, Rebekah and Isaac formed alliances with different children. Such coalitions eventually proved destructive to the family, creating cycles of competition, jealousy, rivalry, and decades-old resentment. Jacob's home never seemed to have quite enough love or attention or approval to go around. His father, Isaac, appeared emotionally unavailable to him. Rebekah consistently related to Esau in a negative way. Esau thus courted his father's love by bringing him choice meats (verse 28). Jacob also yearned for his father's affections. But how could he compete head-to-head with his aggressive, dashing older brother? It's often easier to be attracted to those who are athletic and adventuresome. They're more flashy. Jacob had to get around his physically stronger and flamboyant brother by using his head and playing on his brother's weaknesses. So began a lifelong codependent cycle of meeting physical strength with cunning. Of wrestling! Jacob had to outwit his brother if he was going to get ahead. Behind it all was a sense of unfairness and concern for his status in the family. Through it all he longed for the coveted blessing, the birthright.

The presence or absence of blessing is a prominent theme in Jacob's story. The Jacob-Esau narrative centers on the struggle over blessing as do the Laban-Jacob and Leah-Rachel (as well as the Joseph-10 brothers) portions of the story. As Roop notes: "Blessing, the power for a fruitful, prosperous life, complicates all the stories, pitting the less blessed Esau against the more blessed Jacob, the less fertile Rachel against the more fertile Leah. Being the more blessed does not ensure one's happiness, however, as both Jacob and Leah experience. But neither is there any great pleasure in being the less blessed, as the pilgrimages of Rachel and Esau demonstrate."[11]

Behind it all lurks the need for security and acceptance. "For sons and daughters in biblical times, receiving their father's blessing was a momentous event. . . . It gave these children a tremendous sense of being highly valued by their parents and even pictured a special future for them. As a specific point in their lives they would hear words of encouragement, love, and acceptance from their parents."[12]

We still see it today. "Parents sometimes inflame the relationships among our children by the way we treat them and show our affection. Even when we try to be even-handed, children sometimes feel we are not as close to them as we are to a brother or sister, and then, who better to take out their frustrations on than the object of their jealousy? How many times have we heard one of our kids say, 'How come So-and-so gets to go and I cannot?' Or 'Why is it that you never yell at my sister and only pick on me?'"[13] How many times have I been told of family favorites who get more time, more money, more love, more attention, more breaks? No matter how attentive our parents are, we never get all the approval we crave. Esau's anguished cry, "Do you have only one blessing, my father? Bless me, even me also, O my father" (Gen. 27:38, NKJV), resounds in the heart of every child who has ever felt displaced in his parent's heart by a brother or sister. Esau raised his voice and wept. "Gaining or missing out on parental approval has a tremendous effect on us. . . . What happens in our relationship with our parents can greatly affect all our present and future relationships,"[14] including our view of God and relationship with Him. "For almost all children who miss out on their parents' blessing, at some level this lack of acceptance sets off a lifelong search."[15] In the process even God can be elusive.

Third, Jacob and Esau had differences that went beyond their personalities, beyond their likes and dislikes, and beyond their lop-sided relationship with their parents. They had contrasting moral and spiritual interests and values. We see their divergent values expressed within their struggle for the blessing—the birthright. Esau did not value the birthright more than a bowl of soup. When he spurned his birthright, Esau rejected part of his identity and belittled his destiny. Effectively canceling himself out as a genuine leader in his family, he belittled himself as firstborn. No innocent victim of his brother's conniving, Esau didn't take sufficient care of his birthright. It wasn't that important. Perhaps he even despised it.

Jacob on the other hand valued that birthright and felt himself drawn by the spiritual realities of its spiritual leadership role. *Patriarchs and Prophets* tells us that "Jacob had learned from his mother . . . that the birthright should fall to him, and he was filled with an unspeakable desire for the privileges which it would confer. It was not the possession of his father's wealth that he craved; the spiritual birthright was the object of his longing. To commune with God . . . , to offer the sacrifice . . . , to be the progenitor of the chosen people and the promised Messiah, and to inherit immortal possessions."[16]

Finally, each brother focused on self and meeting his own self-centered ambitions. Each regarded the other as only an obstacle, a competitor, or someone to use to get his way. We often zero in on Esau, who spurned his birthright, but how about Jacob, who rejected his brother? "What about the attitude that says: 'I will give you something only if you give me something first'?"[17] Jacob degraded Esau first within his heart by way of attitudes and thinking and then by action and deception. In the process he ruined himself with envy and manipulation.[18] Jacob knew his brother was a slave to his appetites, and took advantage of those weaknesses for his own benefit. But Esau degraded himself, too. He also took advantage of Jacob when he assumed he could come home and have supper made. They both wound up using each other to get what they wanted, thus regarding the other as only an object to use or circumvent. A means to the end. Although they declared to each other, "I have what you want; you have what I want," at the same time they had no real respectful interchange or personal relationship. Only self and self's agenda. I and it. No I and thou.

In addition, Jacob sought a good thing in a bad way. We cannot praise him for his method. Jacob had his mother on his side, truth on his side, and a better character/lifestyle going for him as well. But just because he had prophecy on his side or what appeared to be the better-chosen lifestyle or even the approval of a parent or authority figure, that did not give Jacob the right to degrade someone else— to covet and take away what the other had.

We have here an incredible image of two brothers going in two different directions but with one common motivation—self.

THEY BOTH MISSED IT

Different personalities, lopsided relationship with parents, contrasting values, self in focus—all are ingredients for conflict, the stuff of family dysfunction.

There can be no resolution at this phase of the story except the knowledge that the narrator provides regarding how God foresees and knows each of Isaac's sons intimately. It will be decades until the rifts between them resolve. However, even at this point in the story we find the promised birthright and what it stood for spiritually and morally in relation to God. One brother desperately wanted the blessing, and the other cared little for it. The fact is that both Esau and Jacob missed its deeper meaning entirely. The missing element in this story is that neither Jacob nor Esau had a relationship with God, something the birthright assumed.

The absence of relationship with God is very clear in Esau. "See to it that no one misses the grace of God and that no bitter root grows up to cause trouble and defile many. See that no one is sexually immoral, or is godless like Esau, who for a single meal sold his inheritance rights as the oldest son. Afterward, as you know, when he wanted to inherit this blessing, he was rejected. He could bring about no change of mind, though he sought the blessing with tears" (Heb. 12:15-17, NIV).

No pagan, Esau grew up in a home full of abundant spiritual advantages, yet he willingly let spiritual matters slide. Scripture calls him "godless." The Greek word used here means "irreligious, worldly, profane." In other words, spiritual things were not all that important to Esau. He envisioned life and enjoyed life without God. His senses were tuned to the physical world around him. One might conclude that he was even a bit cynical or antagonistic when it came to religion. When Scripture says, "See to it that no one misses the grace of God" "or is godless like Esau," it points to a moral spiritual orientation in the context of personal choice and careful decision. We are to care for or look after certain things. The Greek implies it's a continuous responsibility. As with Esau, any of us can miss God's presence and grace altogether or come too late to it because of our own fault. It can happen to you. Maybe it already has. Are you despising your birthright? choosing instead the savory but passing pottage of this world?

But this lack of relationship with God was true for Jacob as well. While he valued eternal things above temporal blessings, he did not have a personal relationship with God: "With secret longing he listened to all that his father told concerning the spiritual birthright; he carefully treasured what he had learned from his mother. Day and night the subject occupied his thoughts, until it became the absorbing interest of his life. But while he thus esteemed eternal above temporal blessings, Jacob had not an experimental knowledge of the God whom he revered. His heart had not been renewed by divine grace. He believed that the promise concerning himself could not be fulfilled as long as Esau retained the rights of the firstborn, and he constantly studied to devise some way whereby he might secure the blessing which his brother held so lightly, but which was so precious to himself."[19]

Ironic, isn't it? We can value spiritual things, be passionately interested in spiritual activities, but have no genuine spiritual experience. Perhaps we know "about" God, but do not know God Himself! We can be a Jacob as easily as we can be an Esau. Each of us needs an experiential knowledge of God. "Eternal life is this," Jesus prayed to His Father, "to know you, the only true God, and Jesus Christ whom you have sent" (John 17:3, New Jerusalem).

Only a relationship with God can temper the potential ingredients for conflict because of differing personality, lopsided parental love, contrasting values, and self-centeredness.

What interpersonal issues are you wrestling with right now? Whom are you at war with? How are you in relation to some other member in your family? Have you stopped to consider and be honest about the kinds of things going on inside yourself that may be driving that conflict or at least keeping the dysfunction alive from your side? The same God who longed for intimacy with Esau and Jacob—knowing He alone could overcome their passionate rivalry and meet their respective needs—longs to bring His grace to work for you. As Scripture says, "See to it that you don't miss it." Let the grace of Jacob's God grip you with transforming power.

---

[1] Gene A. Getz, *Jacob: Following God Without Looking Back* (Nashville: Broadman & Holman, 1996), p. 8.

[2] David Pitt, "Baby Photographed Reaching From Womb," *Associated Press,* Apr. 23, 2000; *Family News From Dr. James Dobson,* April 2000.

[3] Other passages that feature God's perspective on the viability of the unborn as well as in utero influence and development include: Jeremiah 1:5 (Jeremiah); Psalm 139:13-16 (David); Luke 1:15, 44 (John the Baptist); Judges 13:2-7 (Samson)

[4] Getz, p. 10.

[5] Eugene F. Roop, *Genesis* (Scottdale, Pa.: Herald Press, 1987), p. 169.

[6] *Ibid.*

[7] *Ibid.,* p. 165.

[8] *Ibid.,* p. 167.

[9] N. Rosenblatt and J. Horwitz, *Wrestling With Angels,* p. 240.

[10] Ellen G. White, *Patriarchs and Prophets* (Mountain View, Calif.: Pacific Press Pub. Assn., 1958), p. 177.

[11] Roop, p. 166.

[12] Gary Smalley and John Trent, *The Blessing* (New York: Simon & Schuster, Inc., 1986), p. 17.

[13] Norman J. Cohen, *Self, Struggle and Change* (Woodstock, Vt.: Jewish Lights Pub., 1995), p. 99.

[14] Smalley and Trent, p. 11.

[15] *Ibid.,* p. 17.

[16] White, p. 178.

[17] Victor P. Hamilton, *The Book of Genesis: Chapters 18-50* (Grand Rapids: William B. Eerdmans Pub. Co., 1995), p. 186.

[18] Burton L. Visotzky, *The Genesis of Ethics* (New York: Crown Pub., 1996), p. 140.

[19] White, p. 178.

WHEN DAD SAYS YES AND MOM SAYS NO

(Genesis 27)

I t's a simple little rhyme. But it plunges us immediately into the very heart of this next episode in Jacob's life.

Mommy says Yes.
Daddy says No.
That settles it.
We shall go!

That's exactly what happened in Jacob's family, because Mom and Dad didn't see eye-to-eye over the crucial issue of which son should receive the family inheritance and blessing. They were at odds on that momentous question, and so Mom essentially outmaneuvered Dad in order to force her will. Mommy said Yes. Daddy said No. Let's read:

"When Isaac was old and his eyes were so weak that he could no longer see, he called for Esau his older son and said to him, 'My son.' 'Here I am,' he answered. Isaac said, 'I am now an old man and don't know the day of my death. Now then, get your weapons—your quiver and bow—and go out to the open country to hunt some wild game for me. Prepare me the kind of tasty food I like and bring it to me to eat, so that I may give you my blessing before I die.'

"Now Rebekah was listening as Isaac spoke to his son Esau. When Esau left for the open country to hunt game and bring it back, Rebekah said to her son Jacob, 'Look, I overheard your father say to your brother Esau, "Bring me some game and prepare me some tasty food to eat, so that I may give you my blessing in the presence of the Lord before I die." Now, my son, listen carefully and do what I tell you: Go out to the flock and bring me two choice young goats, so I can prepare some tasty food for your father, just the way he likes it. Then take it to your father to eat, so that he may give you his blessing before he dies'" (Gen. 27:1-10, NIV).

Mommy says Yes.
Daddy says No.
That settles it.
We shall go!

In the process a family gets torn apart, wrecked by jealousy, deception, crushed feelings, guilt, deep resentments, and the struggle for power.

AN ORDINARY FAMILY

All the incidents involving Jacob's family will in one way or another touch on either family life or interpersonal dynamics. The Jacob cycle of stories is a classic example of a dysfunctional family. But this particular episode especially zeros in on several critical ethical issues in family life. If you are in touch at all with some of the dysfunctional patterns existing in your own immediate family, the painful cycles you may have experienced in your family growing up, or the debilitating codependent relationships manifesting themselves in a family you know, the more Jacob's story comes to life. The more closely we watch what happens in family life—our families—the more typical Jacob's family becomes.[1] Unfortunately, such too-common family patterns spell trouble.

First, we find the question of power in the dynamics of Isaac and Rebekah's marriage. Who's in charge? Who wears the pants? Who is the real power broker in the family? Dad or Mom? We watch a power struggle going on here. It is a chronic flaw that has haunted their relationship for years.

Years ago I attended a human relations workshop as part of my ministerial training. A weekend designed to develop awareness and personal skills in how to get along with and work with others, it required spouses to participate. During that weekend the instructors divided us into groups of eight that would be permanent for the three-day experience. We almost lived together during the long weekend. Assigned tasks to work on together, we also ate together and spent our free time together. The group I was in comprised four couples. Immediately I sensed that we were in trouble, for five of the eight began jockeying for position from the word go. I sat back and watched three days go by, saying to myself, "What a waste." And doing everything to keep myself from not getting caught up in the pettiness of it all.

It was three days of power struggle with none of the five willing to compromise. Each of them wanted to be leader of the group. They each wanted only their ideas to be accepted, worked on, implemented. Worse yet, they would block some very good ideas simply because one of the others had suggested it. Sometimes two or three would work against the rest of us. At other times the five would struggle against each other. After ganging up to get something across, they would then divide over the next task. A facade of politeness hid feelings of anger and resentment. After all, we were seminary students preparing for ministry—God's servants. Yet the competitive dog-eat-dog undercurrent was both stressful and exasperating.

On the last day we received a box of Tinker Toys to build a structure that would symbolize our shared vision of the ideal church and its ministry in the world. For almost two hours I watched one or two on our team put the blocks together, only to have someone else tear them apart. Each had their reasons for rejecting the previous attempt and would go on to construct what they felt should be the vision. You could feel the tension and confusion.

When the workshop facilitator came around to our group and asked us to share what we had built, we had only a pile of Tinker Toys strewn in the middle of our circle. We looked more like a demolition team than a group of builders. Our group had no fancy-looking creation on display like the others. By now it had become common knowledge that we were a deviant circle. Embarrassed and exasperated, I wanted to hide!

Even as I write this, my mind replays like a video clip two individuals from our team frantically trying to describe what our jumbled pile of Tinker Toys really meant. They were quickly sticking pieces together in bizarre patterns, sheepishly explaining themselves as they attempted to bring order out of our chaos. In the process their teammates repeatedly interrupted them by pulling it all apart again and trying to construct something entirely different. It all took place in front of six other watching groups. Fifty pairs of eyes were riveted on our dysfunction—the result of a struggle for power.

Unable to believe it, I left that weekend feeling sick. It seemed ridiculous that eight adults—ministerial students and their wives, no less—could not accomplish such a simple project as building a church out of Tinker Toys. I began to realize that while it had been a weekend of games, what those games evoked from our lives was so true to life. The struggle for power was more than something to occupy a weekend. To them it was the only game in town. And it is one that tears families to shreds.

"Most people play power games. There are husbands who want power over their wives, and wives try to gain equal power with their husbands. There are children who struggle to free themselves from the control of parents who tyrannize their children."[2] Add all of this to traditional sibling rivalry and all those dynamics that play out in the context of birth order. Having a neurotic need to control, we feverishly seek to manipulate, to be in charge. "Power's ability to destroy human relationships is written across the face of humanity."[3] It's all here in Jacob's family—and ours!

Isaac had his mind set to bless his favored son, Esau. Rebekah, however, "was confident that it was contrary to what God had revealed as His will."[4] Besides, Jacob was her favorite son. In vain she had tried to reason with Isaac. Isaac, though, was unshaken in his determination to bestow upon Esau the birthright even though God had already revealed His will in the matter.[5] In fact, knowing the opposition of both Rebekah and Jacob (and perhaps God) Isaac decided to conduct the solemn ceremony in secret.[6] But Rebekah was skilled at eavesdropping and decided on a plan of her own. "Listen to me as I command you," she ordered Jacob (Gen. 27:8, NASB). "Hey, this is what your dad has said, but I want you to do what I command you to do." In the process both Esau and Isaac got caught up in the power play. Hostages to their parents' marriage—the tensions between Mom and Dad—they merely replicated the power-play dynamics at work in their parents' relationship.

We have already learned how Jacob and Esau grew up under the lopsided love of their parents. Isaac (Dad) loved Esau while Rebekah (Mom) loved Jacob. It is human and, to some degree, inevitable that every parent develops a closer rapport with one child than with another. Unfortunately, we also struggle with the temptation to use our relationship with a favorite child to compensate for emotional disappointments in our marriage or to leverage our way through some family disagreement. Family alliances can be dangerous, unless the alliance is between Mom and Dad. Then the family has a chance. The story of Jacob and Esau is a strong warning of the danger to children when parents draw them into the shifting power balance of their marriage. It was more than a matter of favorites, as we learned in our last chapter. Favorites become pawns, chips to play, crowbars to leverage one's will, or expressions of power.

As Naomi Rosenblatt and Joshua Horwitz say: "Many families that harbor underlying tensions between the mother and father have a tendency to split into two camps. More often than not, family members remain unconscious or in denial of this truth—until circumstances bring the two opposing sides into open conflict. But by that time it is often impossible to prevent a catastrophic head-on collision."[7] The dynamics of a home will reflect the parents' marriage. Power struggles between Mom and Dad can easily become a family power struggle. Young people know how to exploit that situation. Going to Dad for one thing and Mom for another, they instinctively pit their parents' differing perspectives or answers or wishes against one another. In the process one parent usually winds up powerless. Unfortunately, all too often it is the father's leadership or authority that gets undercut or destroyed altogether.

Second, there emerges the marginalizing attitude of disrespect. Rebekah is a strong woman who cleverly works to get what she wants. Whenever she acts, the family changes dramatically. In the biblical story she never speaks directly to Esau, and he loses at every step. Everything she says and does demeans or diminishes him as a person. She always acts in Jacob's behalf. One notices a drivenness in her words with Jacob, an impatience in her instruction. "Listen to me as I command" (verse 8, NASB). "Only obey my voice, and go" (verse 13, NASB).

With her husband, Isaac, Rebekah displays both a private and public split. On the one hand, she covertly aligns herself against both Isaac and Esau. Behind the scenes she's trying to undercut Esau and divide him away from Isaac, or Isaac from both Esau and Jacob. On the other hand, when she addresses Isaac directly, speaking face-to-face with him, you would think they were on the same side. Appealing to their shared values about interfaith marriage, she makes Esau look bad by complaining about the turmoil he has brought into their home by marrying pagan women (verse 46).

Behind the scenes Rebekah acts one way but face to face another. At the bottom of it all lurks an attitude of disrespect and disregard for both Isaac and Esau. The way we treat people—family members—reflects how we view them!

Rebekah's spirit of disrespect for Isaac further manifests itself in her willingness to deceptively maneuver around him to nullify his decisions, and in her encouraging Jacob to do the same. While Jacob didn't readily consent to his mom's proposed plan (verses 11, 12), his subsequent actions mirror her marginalizing attitude. Interestingly, Jacob was reticent at first to go along for two reasons. "What if my father touches me?" he says. "I would appear to be tricking him and would bring down a curse on myself rather than a blessing" (verse 12, NIV). Jacob was afraid that he would appear to be deceiving his father. The Hebrew word used here means to "mock" and appears only one other time in the Old Testament. Scripture uses it to criticize the people of Judah for having ridiculed the prophets (2 Chron. 36:16; the same verse employs two other verbs meaning respectively "despised" and "scoffed at").

Obviously, Jacob understood that a show of disrespect was an intrinsic part of the proposed plan. Deception at the bottom dishonors others in that in giving partial, distorted, exaggerated information or withholding data that they need, we rob them of both the dignity and the ability to make an informed choice. We play God for them.

Jacob's second concern over his mother's proposition revolved around his fear of being cursed if he was found mocking his father. Rebekah, however, stared Jacob down, declaring, "Your curse be on me, my son; only obey my voice, and go" (Gen. 27:13, NASB). In other words, "I'll bear the consequences." Don't worry about the curse. Go ahead and mock! Dad and his opinions are inconsequential!

When one parent undermines the integrity, respect, position, or authority of the other in the eyes of their children or encourages a young person to do things that undermine his or her own respect and obedience for that other parent, it not only affects that young person's respect for that parent but unwittingly for the first parent as well. It warps, too, their attitude toward people generally, including leaders and even God!

Attitudes of disrespect can lead to the marginalizing of family members, bringing them to the point where they have almost no meaningful place anymore in the family. Both Isaac and Esau become marginalized in this story. Isaac is just a feeble, old, blind, and headstrong man ready to die. Not of much importance really, except to make sure the family inheritance and blessing don't get squandered, his family ignores his opinion, because he's a has-been. Rebekah, Jacob, and Esau each look on Isaac with a bit of indifference. They pay attention to him only for what they can get out of him before it's too late.

By the time this episode ends, Esau also finds himself pushed to the edge of the family. Although he deeply wants to belong, he has been marginalized by the others. Once "he had been the son his father loved best. Now he [has] almost no place in the family."[8] Some of it has to do with his marriage to women neither Mom nor Dad approved of. "When Esau was forty years old he married Judith the daughter of Beeri the Hittite, and Basemath the daughter of Elon the Hittite; and they brought grief to Isaac and Rebekah" (Gen. 26:34, 35, NASB). Esau's marriages contradicted the moral, spiritual, and family values held by his parents. Later he tried to correct and restore the family relationships by marrying more suitable women, but it was too late (Gen. 28:8, 9). In the end all the family defined themselves as *not Esau.*

Third, we observe a lack of honest communication. As we have already seen, Isaac wasn't very open about his plan to bless Esau. He was going to transfer the birthright in secret—a private transaction rather than a family event. It would just happen. The rest of the family would then just have to live with it, preventing any opportunity to address the real issues at play. The family would have no chance to talk about it and get things out in the open. A healthy family would have nurtured understanding and communication. It would have taken time to unravel feelings and tensions and fears. And it would have sought God's perspective. But Jacob's family was not a healthy one. And so a significant family moment—one wrought with a host of potentially volatile feelings and expectations—took place. And in the process much, if not everything, would be left untouched, unspoken, uncared for, and unchanged.

Rebekah, too, wasn't open and direct with her thoughts on these important family matters. Rather than openly confronting Isaac with her convictions about what she had overheard, she responded with her own undisclosed plan. She didn't genuinely communicate with Jacob either, but just gave him orders. Soon Jacob too became part of the communication blackout. Later, when Esau threatened to kill Jacob, Rebekah blurred the issue further. She came to Isaac pretending that she was distressed (which she was) about the possibility of Jacob marrying the same kind of women his brother had been associating with. Perhaps Jacob ought to go away for a little while and find a bride from among her relatives. "Rebekah said to Isaac, 'I am tired of living because of the daughters of Heth; if Jacob takes a wife from the daughters of Heth, like these, from the daughters of the land, what good will my life be to me?'" (Gen. 27:46, NASB). In other words, Rebekah used the issue of Esau's marriages as a way to rescue Jacob from danger, giving her favorite son's departure a cover of legitimacy. In the process she subtly shifted the issue. She was neither open nor honest about her real agenda or feelings, leaving much left unspoken. Here was a family that didn't communicate well.

Finally, we have a failure to bring reconciliation after wrenching family conflict. Jacob's story raises important questions about peace-making—the process of sharing feelings, expressing apology, extending forgiveness, and making amends. What usually happens when members of the family have collided with one another? What should be done about it? Who has gotten hurt and why? How does each individual feel about the things that have transpired? Who can no longer look whom in the eye? What should be done about it?

Rebekah saw no need either to make open confession of wrong or to encourage reconciliation on the basis of forgiveness. When she heard that Esau bore a grudge against Jacob, and that he was contemplating murder, she called Jacob in and said, "'Behold your brother Esau is consoling himself concerning you by planning to kill you. Now therefore, my son, obey my voice, and arise, flee to Haran, to my brother Laban! And stay with him a few days, until your brother's fury subsides, until your brother's anger against you subsides and he forgets what you did to him. Then I shall send and get you from there'" (verses 41–46, NASB).

Rebekah figured Esau would cool down in time and forget the whole thing. It appears that she just wanted everything ignored so she could enjoy the fruit of her conniving without the inconvenience of dealing with wounded feelings and making things right. Understandably holding a grudge, Esau was planning murder. Jacob apparently fled without apology or attempting to smooth things over. No one was in the mood for reconciliation or at least willing to take the first step. The raw emotional and spiritual wounds inflicted during this painful family encounter would fester for two decades. Unresolved conflict turned the family on its head, creating years of emotional pain, turmoil, and chronic dysfunction.

Can you imagine the kind of pain Jacob's family experienced? It's not hard to, since it comes so close to home. Families haven't changed very much, have they? The struggle for power. The marginalizing attitude of disrespect for one another. The lack of open and honest communication that would facilitate understanding and closeness. The failure to bring reconciliation when painful conflict has produced raw wounds. All are devastating causes of family failure. They still exist in the homes of people like you and me even though we carry the name Christian.

HIS WAY

We need to explore one more dimension of this episode—doing God's will His way and in His time. At the bottom this story concerns doing what is right in a way that affirms the dignity of the significant people around us and that both waits on God's timing and follows His ways of doing things.

Even though God had already revealed His will to the contrary, Isaac persisted in his determination to bestow upon Esau the birthright. Maybe he didn't really believe the divine message communicated through Rebekah. "But knowing the opposition of Rebekah and Jacob, he decided to perform the solemn ceremony in secret."[9] In doing so he brought into the open the long-festering power struggle over the coveted birthright blessing. His decision to do it "my way" produced incredible family brokenness. Obviously, we create unimaginable tension and brokenness in our family whenever we set aside God's clear will or compromise clear moral or spiritual principles in any way.

Furthermore, we can also instigate tension and brokenness by attempting to accomplish God's purposes for us in our way and in our own time. "Jacob and Rebekah succeeded in their purpose, but they gained only trouble and sorrow by their deception. God had declared that Jacob should receive the birthright, and His word would have been fulfilled in His own time had they waited in faith for Him to work for them. But like many who now profess to be children of God, they were unwilling to leave the matter in His hands."[10] How often we try to make God's way fit our understanding of divine intention. There's really only one way to do God's will—His way and in His own time! Anything else leads only to incredible family pain.

The tragic record is compelling: Esau winds up holding a grudge and hating Jacob (verse 41). Isaac becomes afraid for his life—he literally trembles violently—in light of the possible repercussions that might come from God if, indeed, he blessed the wrong son (verse 33).

Rebekah worries that she will have now lost both sons (verses 42-46). In fact, she does. While she "bitterly repented the wrong counsel she had given her son; it was the means of separating him from her, and she never saw his face again."[11] Jacob loses both personal and family face and escapes for his very life, never to see his mother again. *Patriarchs and Prophets* underscores the intense internal wrestling that this moment of family conflict brought Jacob. "From the hour when he received the birthright, Jacob was weighed down with self-condemnation. He had sinned against his father, his brother, his own soul, and against God. In one short hour he had made work for a lifelong repentance. This scene was vivid before him in afteryears, when the wicked course of his own sons oppressed his soul."[12] Finally, Isaac and Rebekah's troubled marriage became further strained.

What a family!

> *Mommy says Yes.*
> *Daddy says No.*
> *That settles it.*
> *We shall go!*

How is it with you? Who are you wrestling with? And what are you wrestling over? Are you a dominating, controlling person locked in some power struggle in your family? With your spouse? a child? a sibling? a parent? In his book *Husbands Who Won't Lead and Wives Who Won't Follow* James Walker puts his finger on the crucial bottom-line issue: "Control, and who has it, is the ultimate, unspoken question in a marriage [or family] conflict. And when the issue is decided, neither side enjoys the result."[13] Even when one spouse or family member achieves maximum influence over the other(s), victory is only bittersweet.

How is your marriage affecting your parenting and the interpersonal dynamics in your home? What kind of relationship do you have between yourself and your spouse? Are you open and honest? willing to communicate and touch the level of feelings, expectations, desires? Are your words or actions, attitudes or expectations, undermining the respect and dignity of another family member?

What happens in your family when it has experienced a painful clash? How long does it take to make things right? Are painful things or assaulted feelings put off to be forgotten or ignored? Has your heart or someone else's heart closed against another?

Again, who are you wrestling with? And what are you wrestling over?

Jacob's family was quite ordinary in the sense of its being a typical worldly-wise family pursuing its individual goals with secular wisdom. This was true even though it was also a household in which God was working and through whom the Messiah would eventually come. What I desire for us to see is that you and I are called to be different. God does not want us to be *ordinary* families pursuing life and establishing our interpersonal relationships with secular wisdom. He has called us to be *extraordinary* families in whom the power and grace of God are most evident. It's a choice! And a journey.

Scripture invites us to be radically different, to rise to a higher level. "Be subject to one another in the fear of Christ" (Eph. 5:21, NASB). "Wives, submit to your husbands as to the Lord" (verse 22, NIV). "Husbands, love your wives, just as Christ loved the church and gave himself up for her to make her holy" (verse 25, NIV). "Children, obey your parents in the Lord, for this is right. Honor your father and mother" (Eph. 6:1, 2, NASB). "Fathers, do not exasperate your children; instead, bring them up in the training and instruction of the Lord" (verse 4, NIV).

Would you like to belong to a household composed of people who behaved like that? A wife who is willing to follow and allows her husband to lead? Who respects him? A husband who loves his wife as he loves himself and who is concerned for her personhood, dignity, growth, and purity? Willing to sacrifice himself for her? A young person who obeys and honors his or her parents? A father whose life and interchange is an encouragement to his children—a welcome mentor in spiritual and moral things as well as life's basic attitudes? A Christian family in which submission permeates the life of every member on a daily basis?

That's why we need God! When members of the family meet the Lord Jesus and surrender to Him, He becomes the bridge toward becoming extraordinary families. He points the way, because He is the way and empowers us toward that way. Christ is our example in the process of submission. "So if in Christ there is anything that will move you, any incentive in love, any fellowship in the Spirit, any warmth or sympathy—I appeal to you, make my joy complete by being of a single mind, one in love, one in heart and one in mind. Nothing is to be done out of jealousy or vanity; instead, out of humility of mind everyone should give preference to others, everyone pursuing not selfish interests but those of others. Make your own the mind of Christ Jesus: Who, being in the form of God, did not count equality with God something to be grasped. But he emptied himself, taking the form of a slave, becoming as human beings are; and being in every way like a human being, he was humbler yet, even to accepting death, death on a cross" (Phil. 2:1-8, New Jerusalem).

In the midst of all this patriarchal family dysfunction we read the responses of the two who apparently got the worst of it. Embittered, Esau holds a grudge and consoles himself with the plan to get even (Gen. 27:41). Isaac, though, comes to see that in spite of Rebekah's shenanigans and Jacob's deception, God's providence defeated his purpose. The right way would still prevail. God has a way of working all things together for good (Rom. 8:28), including the sins of His own children (Gen. 50:20). So what does Isaac do? He experiences the grip of God constraining him deep down inside. At last he chooses to surrender to God's will and proceeds to bless Jacob a second time. His whole heart is in this blessing. Isaac blesses Jacob more powerfully, more emphatically, than he did at first: "So Isaac summoned Jacob and blessed him; and he gave him this order: 'You are not to marry any of the Canaanite women. Go off to Paddan-Aram, the home of Bethuel your mother's father, and there choose a wife for yourself from the daughters of Laban your mother's brother. May El Shaddai bless you; may he make you fruitful and make you multiply so that you become a group of nations. May he grant you the blessing of Abraham, you and your descendants after you, so that one day you may own the country where you are now living as a stranger—which God gave to Abraham'" (Gen. 28:1-4, New Jerusalem).

While Esau has hardened, Isaac is softened. One continues to wrestle. The other surrenders deep down in his inner private world and begins to finds peace with God and all that has happened.

Family life is always one of choice! The choice to be honest and to affirm the personhood of others in both mind and action. To work at being close by developing better communication skills in which we are open with our feelings, agendas, needs, and expectations. The choice to apologize, to forgive, to make things right sooner than later and find reconciliation. Above all else, it is the choice to follow God in His way and in His time—to be like Jesus.

---

[1] E. Roop, *Genesis,* p. 188.

[2] Anthony Campolo, Jr., *The Power Delusion* (Wheaton, Ill.: Victor Books, 1983), p. 9.

[3] Richard J. Foster, *Money, Sex and Power* (New York: Harper & Row, 1985), p. 176.

[4] E. G. White, *Patriarchs and Prophets,* p. 180.

[5] *Ibid.,* p. 179.

[6] *Ibid.*

[7] N. Rosenblatt and J. Horwitz, *Wrestling With Angels,* p. 244.

[8] Roop, p. 187.

[9] White, p. 179.

[10] *Ibid.,* p. 180.

[11] *Ibid.*

[12] *Ibid.*

[13] James Walker, *Husbands Who Won't Lead and Wives Who Won't Follow* (Minneapolis: Bethany House Pub., 1989), p. 21.

FUGITIVE DREAMERS AND AWESOME PLACES

three

(Genesis 28:10-17)

"Dreaming men are haunted men," so the saying goes.[1] We often dream about the very things that trouble our hearts or fill us with fear. Often we can trace the hidden meanings of dreams to events and anxieties of the preceding day—what Freud described as "the day's residue." We thus dream because our subconscious mind hasn't stopped churning even though we're dead to the world in sleep. Our inner private world goes on working because we're anxious to sort our way through the problem and find resolution. In the process all kinds of bizarre (or benign) images coalesce in our mind, creatively portraying either how we feel, what we fear, or the solution we so desperately yearn for.

Jacob became a haunted man, a fugitive on the run driven by the fear that his angry brother might be lurking in the shadows. He wasted no time in responding to his father's command to "go at once to Paddan Aram" (Gen. 28:2, NIV), recognizing that "Esau's threats to kill him were not idle words (Gen. 27:41). Probably he had seen the results of his brother's temper many times before."[2] Now he was the object of such violent hatred.

Beyond that, Jacob was haunted by his failures and the tormenting guilt and humiliating reality of his own shame. "From the hour he received the birthright, Jacob was weighed down with self-condemnation. He had sinned against his father, his brother, his own soul, and against God. In one short hour he had made work for a lifelong repentance."[3]

So it was with a deeply troubled heart that Jacob set out on his lonely journey to Paddan-aram to find his mother's family. He feared that he had lost forever the blessing that God had purposed to give him. Satan, the great accuser (Rev. 12:10; Zech. 3:1), attempted to discourage, erase all hope, and fill the patriarch's soul with darkness.

Jacob covered nearly 50 miles the first day on the run.[4] Once the sun disappeared over the western hills he stopped for the night. Surrounded by darkness in the lonely wilderness of some unnamed place, he found nothing to soothe his anxious soul, no place to lay his head down: Scripture tells us that Jacob "came to a certain place and spent the night there, because the sun had set; and he took one of the stones of the place and put it under his head, and lay down in that place" (Gen. 28:10, 11, NASB).

If you've ever been in the pitch-black darkness of a wilderness night, it can be a scary experience, especially when you are alone. The night shadows and sounds can be unnerving and downright spooky. We can only imagine how Jacob might have felt as the darkness settled in with deepening shades of blackness. His search for a pillow compounded his angst. Since he had been a spoiled child at home, perhaps it was the first night that he had ever really camped in the wilderness. Whenever we get tired and want to sleep, we want to rest our heads on something comfortable, so we search for a pillow or someone's shoulder. How many times have you attempted to sleep in the back of a car or in an airplane as you've traveled? Trying to find that right place to put your head is difficult, especially while sleeping on the ground outdoors, as those of us who camp and backpack know all too well. Jacob could find only a stone to lay his weary head on. An ordinary, hard, uncomfortable stone for a pillow. As Watchman Nee observes, "His life of discipline had begun."[5]

Everything Jacob experienced physically echoed the existential upheaval taking place deep within his haunted heart. As the darkness of despair pressed upon his godforsaken soul, Jacob longed for an understanding shoulder to lean upon. Utterly lonely, he felt the need of God more than ever before. He needed assurance, hope, peace. Yet Jacob hardly dared to pray. So with bitter tears and deep humiliation he wept out a confession as he wrestled with himself, his sin, images of his family, and his God. He asked for some evidence that God had not utterly forsaken him but still cared. That he was not lost. His burdened heart, though, still did not find relief. No matter how hard he wrestled, he had lost all confidence in himself and God's grace.[6] But then he had only stones for a pillow.

And so he dreamed (verse 12). Jacob slept, but his subconscious mind kept churning in the darkness. "Dreaming men are haunted men." Haunted men wrestle even in their dreams.

How many of us can identify with Jacob? How many of us at some point in our life—maybe even right now—have felt the pain of family life? Perhaps the pain of family conflict that has created the desire to escape, sent us to running away and yearning for more than a stone. How about that dysfunctional relationship that creates guilt or bitterness or shame? That friction that fills our heart with feelings of rejection, anger, and disappointment? Those episodes that leave us lonely, fearful, depressed—our self-worth shot? All because of the things we have said or done or experienced at the hands of others. Family—the very place we are to call home, the very place where we are to find sanctuary, identity, meaning, purpose, and peace—has blown us apart.

We've learned already how Jacob's family was a troubled and dysfunctional family caught up in conflict. Now we find it a family on the move, as well. Whenever we encounter family conflict, we may also observe constant motion. Too often the two dynamics overlap.[7] People flee from one another because of what someone has said or done or left undone and avoided.

Every one of us at some point has been a fugitive dreamer! Running away. Separating. Divorcing. Yearning to escape. All the while longing for peace and wishing that things could be put back together but not knowing how. It's so much easier to shut down, withdraw, leave.

AWESOME PLACES

Some time ago I carefully studied a most intriguing painting by Bev Dolittle. I had come across the arresting western scene while browsing through an art shop in Winter Park, Colorado. It portrays a rugged wilderness setting in which a lone cowboy rides a pale horse along a craggy wooded trail. He's leading a packhorse along behind him. Their trail through the woods has narrowed and sloped downward toward a rushing stream that he is beginning to cross. Everything in the scene has an eerie, chilling feel to it. The artist has filled it with ghostly shadows, creepy shapes, swirling rapids, massive boulders, deep brush, windswept trees, an overcast sky, and blowing leaves.

As the solitary cowboy leads the packhorse across the stream he looks back over his shoulder. But he's not glancing at his packhorse. He's gazing back as if he knows he's being watched or followed. A worried look crosses his ashen face. His one hand hovers near his revolver.

As you keep focusing on the details of the painting, suddenly you observe faces all around the nervous fellow. Camouflaged in the dense foliage, swirling stream, and rugged terrain are 14 Indian faces. They lurk in the contours of trees or hide in the shadows and the rock formations, even the swirling waters. Dolittle has titled the painting *The Forest Has Eyes.*

Jacob went to sleep in a nameless desolate place with his head on an ordinary windswept rock. Haunted by a vision of his failure and feeling alone and forsaken by God, his restless mind kept on working long after his weary body had taken rest. As Jacob dreamed, a stairway appeared linking heaven and earth. Angels went up and down it. The Lord Himself stood at the top of the stairway and spoke words of promise: "'I am the Lord, the God of your grandfather Abraham and the God of your father, Isaac. The ground you are lying on belongs to you. I will give it to you and your descendants. Your descendants will be as numerous as the dust of the earth! They will cover the land from east to west and from north to south. All the families of the earth will be blessed through you and your descendants. What's more, I will be with you, and I will protect you wherever you go. I will someday bring you safely back to this land. I will be with you constantly until I have finished giving you everything I have promised.'

"Then Jacob woke up and said, 'Surely the Lord is in this place, and I wasn't even aware of it.' He was afraid and said, 'What an awesome place this is! It is none other than the house of God—the gateway to heaven!'" (verses 13-17, NLT).

It was no ordinary dream, no subconscious existential conjuring explainable by Freudian psychology. Rather, it was a direct revelation from God—a means that He sometimes used to communicate to people, both believers and nonbelievers (Gen. 40:1-23; Dan. 2:1-49; Acts 10:1-48). It was something that wonderfully overlapped with the natural existential phenomenon of "dreaming men are haunted men."

The stairway linking heaven and earth with its angel messengers was a glorious sight. God Himself stood at the top of the stairs. It was something Jacob desperately longed for but never expected. Here right where he was—in the middle of nowhere and in the middle of his guilt and condemnation—God appeared. The Lord compassionately had revealed just what Jacob needed: a sense of His presence and gracious help in the midst of darkness and despair. With it, the promise of renewal, came restoration and forgiveness.

Unlike the ill-at-ease cowboy who knows he is being watched and followed by lurking enemies, Jacob is both surprised and overwhelmed at the thought that God might be watching and journeying with him. Though it is camouflaged against the outlines of the rugged wilderness terrain he was traveling through as well as the textures of his own rugged family dysfunction and personal failure, Jacob still sees God's face. When the face of God emerges in a place that appeared barren and painful, the patriarch can only exclaim, "God is in this place, and I didn't even know it. *This is an awesome place!*" (see Gen. 28:16, 17).

Six times this relatively brief but very important episode uses the Hebrew term for "place": "He came to a certain *place* . . . ; and he took one of the stones of the *place* . . . and lay down in that *place*. . . . 'Surely the Lord is in this *place*.' . . . 'How awesome is this *place*.' . . . He called the name of that *place* Bethel" (verses 11-19, NASB). *Place* is a key word.[8] It points beyond mere physical or geographic location to what happens there to make it unique and forever memorable. "*A certain place* is now experienced as God's place."[9] He is here in the middle of nowhere and in the midst of my wrestling.

Wherever we find God, it's an awesome place!

Revelation opens a window for us into the awesome heavenly throne room where God sits on His majestic emerald throne. There, surrounded by 24 elders, four living creatures, and seven lamps of billowing fire, innumerable angels exclaim His holiness and proclaim His right to receive glory and honor and power and blessing. Scripture portrays God's infinite distance through the imagery of a throne placed in the midst of a shimmering crystal sea and the heavenly host prostrating themselves in adoration and praise. The throne room of God is an awesome place that elicits reverence, awe, and worship (Rev. 4; 5). But it is just as awesome to find God present in the midst of our brokenness, guilt, shame, and family dysfunction. Perhaps it is even more awesome. "This is an awesome place!" we should exclaim in the midst of our wrestling. "I didn't know God was here."

Can we ever get away from God even when we have sinned or blown it? plummeted to the bottom? No. There is no depth too low, no height too high, no place too distant or too secluded to be without God. No sin or failure on our part, no family dysfunction can separate us from God's love. The Lord stands with us even in the darkness of our family anguish.

"I can never escape from your spirit!
  I can never get away from your presence!
If I go up to heaven, you are there;
  If I go down to the place of the dead, you are there.
If I ride the wings of the morning,
  if I dwell by the farthest oceans,
even there your hand will guide me,
  and your strength will support me.
I could ask the darkness to hide me
  and the light around me to become night—
  but even in the darkness I cannot hide from you.
To you the night shines as bright as day.
  Darkness and light are both alike to you" (Ps. 139:7-12, NLT).
Wonderful, isn't it? Most of the time we either don't believe it,

are unaware of it, or can't feel it or see it. When we've had that argument, that difficulty, that ongoing power struggle, lopsided relationship, or episode of falsehood or manipulation—whatever it is!—at that moment we don't realize God is there. We see only the problems and how we're being treated or how we now regret what we've said or done or felt. At such moments our failures and problems overwhelm us and block our spiritual vision. But nevertheless, even in the ordinariness of everyday family experience, God is still there. Whenever we catch a glimpse of that amazing truth, our response will be the same: "This is an awesome place!"

Scripture plays on the theme of place and rock.[10] A nameless place and an ordinary rock become the site where God meets us in our greatest need. When we're on the run after some great family blowout, or some private thing we've done that our family may not even know about—the ordinariness of family conflict—we can be sure God is running along with us.

Jacob saw in that dream exactly what he needed—a Saviour. He had sinned, but his heart rejoiced that a way existed by which he could be restored to God's favor—the ladder, the stairway. A connection existed between himself and heaven.

That mystic ladder is the same that Jesus referred to when He said: "You will see the heavens opened and angels of God ascending and descending on the Son of Man" (John 1:51, NASB). Jesus consciously draws imagery from Jacob's awesome dream to make a radical claim about Himself. Jesus Himself is that vital connecting link between heaven and earth. The stairway ladder is an image of His incarnation—His becoming one with us in our humanity so that He can be touched with our feelings, understand our weaknesses and trials, and extend compassionate mercy and grace when we've fallen. Because He became like us in all things and has gone through suffering and temptation, Jesus is able to strengthen us when we face temptation. He can help us to be strong when we need it the most (Heb. 2:14-18; 4:14-16). Having become one with us in our sorrows and trials, Jesus ministers for us in heaven as our great high priest.

That stairway, then, depicts the incarnate Christ linking heaven with the bottomless pit of dysfunction, failure, brokenness, guilt, and low self-worth that we experience in family. It also symbolizes how the merits of Jesus and His work on the cross connect heaven and earth together as well. Through His death Jesus enables us who are broken and sinful and fragmenting to receive forgiveness from sin and cleansing power to become both a new family member and a new family. Through His cross Jesus bridges the gulf of sin, uniting us in our weakness and helplessness with the source of infinite power.

This is what our soul needs when we are weary with family problems or get caught up in a power struggle. Whether we know we haven't been truthful or fully open or our attitude needs adjusting. Whether we have been bruised or have done the wounding. Whether we want healing or want to make things right. At moments like these we long for the power that only God can provide.

Jacob's dream assures us of God's presence and power in the midst of our brokenness. When I read this story, it encourages me that hope exists not only for ourselves as individuals, but for our families—and for all our interpersonal relationships. As I read the account, I find myself asking, "How do we find God?" After all, that's what Jacob yearned for—to find God. But do we find Him? Or does He search us out? Does the way we speak to ourselves deep inside (that existential wrestling) have something to do with the manner God reveals Himself to us? I think so! This is where we can come to experience the grip of God most keenly. And that very inner wrestling can be heartening proof of His presence.

THE SLOW CLIMB

What is interesting to me is what Jacob does with the place and the stone once he grasps the reality that it was indeed an awesome place. He awakens in the morning and responds to his incredible encounter with God. His words pick up on the key word *place* and his actions involve the second key word *stone:* "So Jacob rose early in the morning, and took the stone that he had put under his head and set it up as a pillar and poured oil on its top. He called the name of that place Bethel" (Gen. 28:18, 19, NASB). We find him naming the place where he camped and pouring oil on the stone on which he slept. He sets the stone up as a pillar, a personal memorial of what God was doing for him. Next he renames the place to celebrate God's gracious presence and promise. The nameless place becomes the house of God (Bethel), and the ordinary stone a sacred pillar. Jacob attaches meaning to the geographical and the tangible. Symbolism becomes an important link between his experience and his response, between his memory and his being and doing.

In gratitude Jacob then promises to be faithful to his God who shows such grace and love. "Then Jacob made a vow, saying, 'If God will be with me and will watch over me on this journey I am taking and will give me food to eat and clothes to wear so that I return safely to my father's house, then the Lord will be my God and this stone that I have set up as a pillar will be God's house, and of all that you give me I will give you a tenth'" (verses 20-22, NIV).

It is not a bargain with God. Jacob isn't sitting back and saying, "God, I tell You what. I'll pay tithe [his last promise, by the way], and I'll call You my God if you give me clothes to wear and You bring me back home and You put everything back together." That's not how we read these verses. God has already revealed Himself and promised the patriarch as much. And more! In fact, God makes it all very personal. "I will give" you the land I promised to your grandfather Abraham and your father Isaac (verse 13, NIV). "Behold, I am with you and will keep you wherever you go, and will bring you back to this land; for I will not leave you until I have done what I have promised you" (verse 15, NASB). Notice all those "I's" on God's lips. The only condition in the equation is our choice to allow God to do in our lives what He wants to do and has promised to do! The Lord will not forsake us. And so we have this image of a man overwhelmed with the compassionate presence and gracious power of God in the midst of his family brokenness. Jacob says to Him, "OK! If this is the kind of God You are going to be, then You are going to be my God! Not only are You going to be my God, but I am going to show it in a tangible way through how I use my resources and material wealth."

That's what tithing points to. It has nothing to do with finances but everything to do with saying, "You're my God. My life is Yours now!"

So we find commitment and renewal. Now Jacob finds rest and peace in the promise of God. The vow reorients his journey. His fugitive flight now becomes pilgrimage. Jacob has committed himself to living with Yahweh as his God. "From the cross of Calvary, Christ calls for an unreserved consecration. All that we have, all that we are, should be devoted to God."[11] When that occurs, we will no longer need stone pillows!

At Bethel God reveals Himself as with us in our pain and brokenness. And Jacob reorients himself in light of that awesome reality. Interestingly, though, in spite of God's gracious presence and Jacob's heartfelt commitment, the patriarch does not suddenly change in character. Nor does he receive a quick resolution to his family problems. The conflict, pain, and confusion remain despite the dream. Jacob bows, commits himself to God, and declares, "I'll pay a tithe." But that doesn't solve family problems. It will take 20 more years before Jacob brings some resolution to part of his family struggle. And his mother dies in the meantime, so he never has an opportunity to bring any closure or reconciliation with her. Twenty more years . . . and some things never do get cared for. And yet Jacob now lives as one who carries God's promise of family renewal.[12]

Even though in the midst of our brokenness God comes with a promise that we accept, it doesn't suddenly rectify everything. But it does mean that we can begin living and going in the direction God wants us to with hope and confidence. It enables us to journey toward that promise of family healing with peace, not condemnation.

Have you seen the abbreviated saying PBPWMGHFWMY. (Please be patient with me; God hasn't finished with me yet)? That's where we are with Jacob at this juncture in his story. It would be a "slow climb out of despair." Wounded hearts, shattered relationships, or cycles of dysfunction cannot be undone in a minute or by a single prayer. Sometimes it takes a lifetime. As Ellen White says: "In one short hour he [Jacob] had made work for a lifelong repentance. This scene was vivid before him in afteryears, when the wicked course of his own sons oppressed his soul."[13] And Rebekah? She "bitterly repented the wrong counsel she had given her son; it was the means of separating him from her, and she never saw his face again."[14] Did the Lord forgive her? Of course! But did it change circumstances and remove the pain? No!

I received a six-page letter from a mother in the church I pastor, someone who shares regularly with me (usually in writing) about her painful journey with family. Often it is in response to things she has heard me say from the pulpit. Sometimes it flows out of the raw emotions stirring in her wounded soul—how she blames herself for past choices and not being able to live the Christian life she wants to. It's tough trying to be the Christian woman God wants her to be in a non-Christian home where she seems to fail so miserably and so often. Most of the time she doesn't ask for or need a response, but just shares her journey, her struggle, her musings. She has even given me permission to use anything she shares (on condition of anonymity) as an illustration in my preaching. "I have learned in the past that if one opens up to others," she once wrote, "they can use it as a learning experience to serve others."

In her letter she describes coming to church one Sabbath feeling intensely alone, abandoned, and in need, because of what was taking place in her family as well as her own failures and inadequacies. In fact, she almost didn't come at all that day. She writes: "Human beings are very delicate creations of God, and when they are hurt, they become even more delicate and need nurturing and loving care. This is where I am at right now and have been praying about how I'm feeling and for some meaning and direction at this point in my life. . . . I came to church feeling very down and very much alone. I then told myself to focus on someone else and also reminded myself that life could be worse. When you came up and started talking to me, this is what I was thinking. You didn't say much, but you made a difference in my day because of what you said. If that was not enough to show me that God cares about even the least of us, Kathy talked to me after Sabbath school about things I could really relate to. Afterward I didn't feel quite so bad. If that still wasn't enough, Freda questioned me a little bit and we talked briefly about my kids. Out of the blue she said to call her any time, that she wouldn't mind being a spiritual mentor for me.

"Once I got out of the church parking lot, I took the long way home and spent a lot of time crying as I am doing now. I just can't get over how good God is and how He takes over at every point in my life to fill every need that I have. . . . I made a conscious choice to be there today, and the Lord fed and cared for me while I was there through the people I have mentioned, and you all don't even know that you were an answer to prayer."

Like Jacob, she came with feelings of guilt and failure. "God, there is so much dysfunction and wounding in my family. What am I going to do about it? The reality of my sinful choice is in front of me every day of my life, and the thought that my kids may be lost because of this choice is unbearable! Please give me some indication that You are with me in spite of what I have said and done. That You are at work in my family in spite of myself." And God reveals Himself and answers her prayer. The stairway is still there—for her and for you and for all our families.

Jacob wrestled with the same kinds of things—the interpersonal conflicts, the deep sense of failure and inadequacy, the confusion and pain, the crying out for God—that we struggle with!

I closed the last chapter by asking some tough questions about where we are in our marriages and family relationships. How is it with you and your family? Are you a dominating person locked in some power struggle for control in your family? How is your marriage affecting your parenting and interpersonal dynamics in your home? Are you open and honest? Or are you undermining the respect and dignity of another family member? What happens in your family after a painful clash? How long does it take to make things right? Do you shove painful things or feelings in with the rest of the skeletons in your family closet?

Right now I want to hold out the promise that no matter where you are on these issues God's presence is still with you. He loves you and your family. The stairway still links human hearts to heaven. It can connect your heart to heaven right now.

When the pain of life puts you on the run, you can find hope in the gracious presence of our compassionate God. Should you be a fugitive dreamer—yearning in your heart for peace, reconciliation, forgiveness, a second chance, or renewing power—you too can encounter awesome places. God will reveal Himself to you.

---

[1] B. Moyers, *Genesis: A Living Conversation*, p. 275.

[2] G. Getz, *Jacob*, p. 56.

[3] E. G. White, *Patriarchs and Prophets*, p. 180.

[4] Getz, p. 56.

[5] Watchman Nee, *The God of Abraham, Isaac and Jacob* (Anaheim, Calif.: Living Stream Ministry, 1995), p. 118.

[6] *Ibid.,* p. 119.

[7] E. Roop, *Genesis,* p. 167.

[8] *Ibid.,* pp. 191, 192.

[9] *Ibid.,* p. 192.

[10] *Ibid.,* p. 191.

[11] White, p. 188.

[12] Roop, p. 194.

[13] White, p. 180.

[14] *Ibid.*

WAKING UP TO REALITY
four

(Genesis 29:15-30)

Jacob's wedding is the kind of tale that raises disturbing and haunting questions. After seven years of anxious waiting, Jacob finally gets to marry the love of his life. But when he wakes up the next morning he finds he's been sleeping with someone totally different than he thought he had married. How in the world could something like that ever happen? You would think that sometime during that night he would have realized that the woman he was embracing was not the one he thought he had married.

Why wasn't he able to tell whom he was making love with? Were there no burning oil lamps to illuminate the scene, no words spoken between them? Were Leah and Rachel somewhat alike in size and build so that it would be hard to tell them apart in the darkness? Did Leah dress up in Rachel's clothing and wear her perfume?

Maybe Jacob wasn't in complete control of his faculties. Genesis tells us that Laban threw a big party to celebrate the moment. He "gathered all the people of the place together, and gave a banquet" (Gen. 29:22, New Jerusalem). The Hebrew word for banquet is *mishteh,* meaning "to drink." So Laban served them all manner of food and wine. Undoubtedly Jacob ate and drank his fill. After all, it was his big day, something he had waited for and worked hard for for seven years. When the evening's festivities wound down, Jacob may have been thoroughly drunk when he went off to his tent to find Rachel—intoxicated by wine and erotic images of love.

"Did he not know the sisters at all, or was he simply so self-involved that he could not distinguish one from the other?"[1]

However we answer such questions—including Leah's complicity in the whole affair—what we do know is that when the morning light dawned in that desert tent, "behold, it was Leah!" (Gen. 29:25, NASB). We can only imagine how utterly aghast Jacob must have been when he looked over and saw Leah. As in the growing light he recognized her face, his heart must have died.

How in the world could something like that ever happen? Maybe it's not all that hard to figure out when we stop to think about it. "After all, Jacob himself had succeeded in usurping his brother's blessing by tricking his blind father only years before."[2] Now, in the dark of his tent with her face likely covered with a veil and wearing Rachel's clothing and perfume—as animal skins had disguised Jacob's neck and arms and he too wore the odorous clothing of Esau—Leah stepped into her sister's place. "In essence, Jacob was as blind as his father. Just as Jacob convinced Isaac that he was the firstborn child, so Laban substituted his firstborn as Jacob's wife."[3] Some translate the reference to Leah's eyes as being "weak." Perhaps "as Jacob stole the blessing because Isaac's eyes were weak, so weak-eyed Leah became his first wife."[4] "Like his father, Isaac, before him, Jacob was blind to the machinations of others."[5] He did not even see who he's making love to. "One imagines him groping in the darkness, like his father . . . did once."[6]

Undoubtedly Jacob had assumed that he was going to marry the love of his life and live happily ever after. But from this day on his life would be only sorrow and incredible pain as he woke up to reality.

It happens all the time! We think that we're seeing clearly, that we know what we want and are reaching for or doing. But that shattering moment arrives when what we thought we saw is in reality something totally and tragically different. It takes place constantly in marriage. Many times as a pastor through the years I have had someone tell me, "I knew the next day. I knew the next day that I had made a mistake." Or "I had known within a year that this person I had married was not the person I thought they were." Even after many years some of us look back and say, "I didn't know this was what I was getting myself into or who this person I married was." Whether it involves friendships or business ventures, at first everything seems so rosy, so promising, and it is moving along in a wonderful way. Then it turns sour, becoming the exact opposite of what we imagined. Maybe it's something we're getting ready to purchase or an entertainment event or a mood-altering substance or a relationship that has grown physical.

Suddenly we wake up to reality and what we thought we were seeing is not there at all. Talk about wrestling!

HONEY TRAPS AND BLIND ALLEYS

What made Jacob so vulnerable? How did he get caught in a trap that cost him 20 years of his life and led to a lifetime of painful family struggle?

First, we must remember the bewitching power of love, the force of emotions and feelings or some consuming desire that can blind us from seeing things as they really are. This episode in Jacob's life is a classic "boy meets girl" love story in which a guy falls head over heels for a girl.

It all began when Jacob arrived at a well near Haran. His personal encounter with God at Bethel had so buoyed his spirits that he literally "picked up his feet" (as the Hebrew reads) with a new sense of motivation "and went to the land of the people of the east."[7] The New Living Translation declares that "Jacob hurried on" (Gen. 29:1). He sped across the next 400 miles not because he feared Esau so much as he was eager to see God's purposes carried out in his life. And he was looking for a wife! When he arrived in the vicinity of Haran, Jacob showed up at a well where a few shepherds were waiting with their flocks. Friendly and cordial, they answered his questions directly and openly.

"'Where do you live?'

"'At Haran,' they said.

"'Do you know a man there named Laban, the grandson of Nahor?'

"'Yes, we do,' they replied.

"'How is he?' Jacob asked.

"'He's well and prosperous. Look, here comes his daughter Rachel with the sheep.'

"'Why don't you water the flocks so they can get back to grazing?' Jacob asked 'They'll be hungry if you stop so early in the day.'

"'We don't roll away the stone and begin watering until all the flocks and shepherds are here'" (verses 4-8, NLT).

Imagine Jacob's emotional reaction when he discovered the shepherds were from Haran and that his long journey was almost over.

In the midst of the conversation Rachel arrived with her father's sheep. Scripture doesn't say how far away she was when the men identified her as Laban's daughter. Nor does it tell us all that was going on in Jacob's heart as she approached. The shepherds had stated that she was Laban's daughter, and Jacob had come to find a wife from within the man's family. Now, here came Rachel, and she met him at a well. Jacob had to be wondering if she was the girl he would eventually marry. Certainly he knew the story of how Rebekah had come to the well near Haran—years ago now—and met Abraham's chief servant, Eliezer. He had journeyed there to find a wife for Jacob's father, Isaac, and his mother, Rebekah, of course, was the woman who had appeared at the well.

Surely Jacob's emotions were running wild, to say the least. And from the moment he set eyes on Rachel, he was in love. You can tell by what he did. First, Jacob tried to get the shepherds to leave so he could be alone with her: "Why don't you water the flocks so they can get back to grazing? . . . They'll be hungry if you stop so early in the day" (verse 7, NLT). Whatever Jacob's thoughts at this moment, he obviously wanted an opportunity to get acquainted with Rachel without a group of shepherds looking over his shoulder and whispering among themselves about this unusual encounter between two cousins who had never met before.

Then in great show of masculine strength, Jacob jumped up, ran to the well, singlehandedly rolled away the huge stone covering the well, and watered Rachel's sheep (verse 10). Such an adrenaline rush clearly indicates his emotional state. He wanted to do something for her. As soon as he had completed the task, Jacob kissed her and began to weep aloud at the joy of finding such a place (verse 11). Obviously, at this point his emotions boiled over. Clearly he had lost control of himself.

Think for a moment about all the things Jacob had been through by now. Through trickery he had usurped his brother's birthright and made a mockery of his aging, blind father. Then he had run away from home because his brother threatened to kill him. As a fugitive dreamer he had come painfully face to face with himself and his deceptions. But he also unexpectedly encountered God and found himself awed by divine grace and promise. Furthermore, Jacob just met a beautiful woman he might one day marry. It had been a roller-coaster ride of experience and emotion. Embarrassing or not, Jacob let go of his emotions. He broke down and wept audibly and publicly.

The unfolding story reveals Rachel's excitement as she ran to tell her father. Laban excitedly rushed out to welcome Jacob with warm hospitality, inviting him home and offering him a place to stay and work to do. In the midst of all the exuberance Jacob couldn't hold it in. He blurted out to Laban the details of what had happened. "Jacob told him his story" (verse 13, NLT).

A month slipped by apparently without any discussion about any financial obligations for either Jacob's room and board or his work. So Laban suggested, "You shouldn't work for me without pay just because we are relatives. How much do you want?" (verse 15, NLT). Though Laban's suggestion sounds generous, we will learn that he was definitely manipulating Jacob. Not wanting to be obligated in any way to his nephew, he maneuvered himself into a position of control. "Before Laban raised the issue of wages, [though] Jacob had been doing some thinking on his own."[8] When he moved into his uncle's home, he discovered that Laban had two daughters, Leah the older, and Rachel, the younger. "Leah had weak [Heb. "delicate, tender, dainty"] eyes, but Rachel was lovely in form, and beautiful" (verse 17, NIV). Apparently Leah had lovely eyes but could not compare in total beauty with Rachel. "From the day they met at the well, Jacob found himself attracted to Rachel, and his feelings of affection had grown stronger during the month that followed."[9]

Now "Jacob was in love with Rachel" to the point that he said, "'I'll work for you seven years in return for your younger daughter Rachel.' Laban said, 'It's better that I give her to you than to some other man. Stay here with me.' So Jacob served seven years to get Rachel, but they seemed like only a few days to him because of his love for her" (verses 18-20).

Did Jacob understand the local custom that a father always gave his oldest daughter in marriage first? If he didn't, Jacob was obviously blind to the reality that "Laban was no doubt already devising a plan to deceive him and to take advantage of his love for Rachel."[10] If he did, then Jacob was likely hoping to work around the custom by appealing to Laban's materialistic interests. His proposed seven years of labor for Rachel's hand in marriage was a good deal for Laban! "Jacob knew that Laban wasn't about to come out on the losing end of this deal. This helps explain his generous offer and why he was willing to be so magnanimous with his time and energy. . . . Jacob had clearly calculated the kind of 'wages' that would entice Laban to look the other way when it came to social customs. Since Jacob loved Rachel so much, he was willing to make this personal sacrifice."[11]

Unfortunately, his love for Rachel blinded him to time, work, and even his uncle's customs. But when he woke up in bed with Leah seven years later, Jacob learned he had calculated wrong.

The bewitching power of love, the force of emotions and feelings, or some consuming desire can unwittingly prevent us from seeing things as they really are. And the result is interpersonal or family dysfunction and intense personal loss and pain.

In her hard-hitting book *How Could You Do That?! The Abdication of Character, Courage, and Conscience,* Laura Schlessinger notes that the number one response she gets from people who call into her syndicated radio program or write her letters about her "reminders of cause and effect, common sense, values, ethics, morality, and fair play is: 'Yeah, I know, but . . .'"[12] In other words, they acknowledge that what she has to say about ethics or values or choices, and consequences is true ("Yeah, I know all that, but . . ."), but then go on to rationalize their action by saying, "But . . . I was . . . well . . . unhappy or confused or frightened, in love, scared to risk, uncomfortable, feeling lonely, feeling needed, feeling anxious, carried away, vulnerable, unawares, victimized." In the middle of this list of excuses Schlessinger inserts an interesting parenthesis: "By the way, by using the word *feeling,* most people think they are now on sacred ground, since pop psych has elevated feelings from information to irresistible force."[13]

Some relationship we're in, some emptiness we long to have filled, or some consuming passion to be someone or do something or have something—they all can blind us. Then comes the searing light of reality.

The second way we can be unwittingly blinded from seeing things as they really are is our tendency to look on the surface of things and not dig deeper into moral or spiritual issues. Genesis tells us that "Leah's eyes were delicate, but Rachel was beautiful in form and appearance" (verse 17, NKJV). Rachel was stunning, and Leah simply could not stand up in comparison. She was just too ordinary. Smitten by Rachel's beauty, Jacob hardly noticed Leah. Perhaps he was so caught up with Rachel's physical presence—how she looked—that he never took the time to really get to know her personally, her character or spiritual interests. For seven years he simply longed for Rachel to the point that his body ached.

Surface beauty is often deceptive. "We, like Jacob, . . . are frequently enticed by what our eyes see and our hearts feel, as opposed to that which our minds and souls can appreciate. We, too, get taken in by surface traits and rarely ever probe"[14] to the deeper levels of values, motives, character, and spiritual interests. Our contemporary generation puts heavy emphasis on appearances: legs, muscles, shape, skin tone. Such focus on appearances goes beyond the human physical body. It includes cars, architecture, icons, marketing, media, even the way things are designed and manufactured. How many of us have purchased a particular item because of the way it looked or felt. We had a similar item to choose from. Both did the same thing, accomplished the same goal. But one had the better feel—better aesthetics.

I find it curious that Genesis later mentions Rachel's theft of

Laban's "household idols" (Gen. 31:19). Having had enough of Laban's manipulative selfishness, Jacob decided to take his wives and leave. As he's packing to slip away secretly, Rachel sneaks out and steals "the household idols that were her father's" (NASB). Why does the biblical record include this little piece of information? What point does it make within the story? The beautiful Rachel steals the family idols. When she's packing to leave, she wants to take the family idols with her. Do Rachel's actions reveal a character weakness?[15] Are we to read between the lines that she may not have been all that interested in Jacob's God? that her heart inclined toward her contemporary culture and its gods? Is it possible that despite all her beauty she was not very deep or spiritual? Did the less glamorous Leah have more substance and spirituality? There's hint of it later.

Perhaps Jacob was so enamored by Rachel's physical presence that he never got serious about her character—what she was really like deep inside. Have similar experiences happened to you? Don't we so often look on the surface and ignore the things that really count when it comes to relationships? In *Patriarchs and Prophets* we read that "it is often the case that persons before marriage have little opportunity to become acquainted with each other's habits and disposition, and, so far as everyday life is concerned, they are virtual strangers when they unite their interests at the altar. Many find, too late, that they are not adapted to each other, and lifelong wretchedness is the result of their union."[16] It's Jacob's story.

Finally, we become blind to reality when we focus on our own ideas and our own plans instead of God's will and God's way. We've all seen movie scenes in which the camera focuses in on an individual's face while completely blurring everyone else. Camera operators can take a shot that puts everyone in focus or they can concentrate on one individual or object and leave everything else a blur. They can even shift our point of view from one character to another, and as they do, we can see the second character sharpen into focus while the first fades away. The same happens with trifocal glasses. Each area of the lenses allows for specific focused vision while everything around remains blurred. Proverbs tells us that "there is a way which seems right to a man, but its end is the way of death" (14:12; 16:25, NKJV). The biblical book is talking about self-made plans—what looks good to us. The course we've outlined for our lives. "Our" plan for the future.

Genesis gives the distinct impression that Jacob had his own ideas about how things should work out in Haran: "Jacob saw Rachel the daughter of Laban his mother's brother, and the sheep of Laban his mother's brother" (Gen. 29:10, NKJV). He was like most young men. First, he sees the girl. Then he notices the car she is driving.[17] I can almost imagine Jacob thinking that he will do just fine here at Laban's place. After all, it had gorgeous Rachel and all Uncle Laban's sheep. Beautiful women combined with lots of money—sweet! "This isn't a bad place at all. I'll make a go of it here for sure. Perhaps it wasn't so bad after all that I had to leave Mom and Dad."

But Jacob's self-made plans and narrowed focus eventually unraveled. In time he experienced two major reversals. He wanted to marry Rachel, but Laban tricked him with Leah. Although devastated, Jacob decided he was going to go for Rachel anyway. To do so he chose the path of polygamy—keeping Leah and marrying Rachel within a week—sisters, no less, something Scripture later condemned: "Do not take your wife's sister as a rival wife and have sexual relations with her while your wife is living" (Lev. 18:18, NIV). A terrible marital beginning for both Leah and Rachel, it became even more complicated by the fact that Jacob "loved Rachel more than Leah" (Gen. 29:30, NIV). It set the stage for family problems that would fester and linger for years to come. In addition, Jacob worked another seven years for Laban (verses 27, 30).

Jacob's second goal was to build a family through Rachel. The problem, though, was that she seemed unable to conceive. Her sister, Leah, was highly fertile: "Now the Lord saw that Leah was unloved, and He opened her womb, but Rachel was barren" (Gen. 29:31, NASB). Obviously, Jacob's lack of love for Leah didn't keep him out of her tent! Whatever his motives—sexual gratification or duty—he did not reject her totally. Think about it, though. He had sex without love, yet the heirs came! On the other hand, his love for Rachel led only to barrenness.

A few years ago I received two e-mail messages in the same week from individuals asking what I knew about the Lichtenwalter family name. One query came from Atlanta, Georgia, the other from Obermoegershiem, Germany, 30 miles (50 kilometers) south of Nuremberg. The fellow in Atlanta was tracing his mother's Lichtenwalter heritage back to Pennsylvania. Did I have any information? The writer in Germany told me of the Lichtenwalters' move from Austria to Germany in the sixteenth century and how his family had lived in the same place for nearly 400 years. He even had documents to prove it. When did the Lichtenwalters emigrate from Germany to America? he wondered. Did I know? When I asked my dad about the two out-of-the-blue inquiries, he point-blank reminded me that the Lichtenwalter branch of the tree that he and I are on had ended with my grandfather Albert. Dad and his sisters had received the Lichtenwalter name when his single-parent mother married Albert Lichtenwalter. His half-brother, William, who had been born through that union, never had children. So this branch of the real Lichtenwalter bloodline dead-ended right there! Neither of us had had a part in it. "Oh well," I mused out loud, "you and I can start our own tree!"

Jacob was dead-ending too! His plans for family with Rachel vanished in emptiness. It is a significant part of the biblical plot, raising existential issues in Jacob's scheming heart. Barrenness is the Bible's metaphor for dead ends and human hopelessness. When human beings reach that point, they no longer have any foreseeable future. Our human power to invent the future and make it beautiful and full of life and laughter comes up empty again and again. By the way, barrenness is the pattern of world history. The end-run of our fallen world. The reality of human life and being. In the end we have no power within us to make a better world or future or save ourselves. We're traveling down a dead-end road.[18]

It is at first surprising to read that the Lord was behind Rachel's barrenness. During that stairway dream, hadn't God promised that Jacob's seed would be as numerous as the dust of the earth (Gen. 28:14)? Now, however, Rachel, his intended wife and the love of his life (Gen. 29:30), could not have children, and it appeared to be the Lord's doing (verse 31). Jacob read as much between the lines too. Later Rachel came to him, begging him for a child: "Give me children, or I'll die," she cried (Gen. 30:1, NLT). "Jacob flew into a rage. 'Am I God?' he asked. 'He is the only one able to give you children'" (verse 2, NLT). The patriarch understood that God had His hand in all this. The twist in the story was Scripture's way of showing "again that Jacob's plans come to naught."[19] What Jacob intended was not necessarily what God had in mind. Jacob had planned to take Rachel as his wife, but one almost gets the impression that the Lord had intended Jacob to marry Leah.

Both women became mothers of sons who stood out from Jacob's other children. Leah gave birth to Judah and Rachel to Joseph. "God used both [sons] in important ways, but each had a different role to play in the accomplishment of God's blessing."[20] Eventually, though, Judah, Leah's son, received the place of prominence, the one through whom the Messiah ultimately came. "Counter to Jacob's plan, God had opened the womb of Leah and not Rachel. . . . God had withheld sons from Rachel so that the seed of Abraham would be built from Leah."[21] As I've already said, one almost gets the impression that God had wanted Jacob to marry Leah instead of her sister.

How are we to read all this except to sense that maybe Jacob was running ahead of God, trying to secure the blessing on his own? Attempting to find the good life in his own way, he had assumed that God would automatically add His blessing to whatever he had in mind without his making any serious attempt to discover God's will or timing.

Our families endure so much pain and we experience so much sorrow in our own lives because we have done things casually or off the cuff. Barrenness is again and again the sequel to not seeking divine guidance seriously.

WHEN DREAMS CRUMBLE

Waking up to reality, Jacob realized that love and feelings and outward appearances had led him down a dead end. His own ideas and plans had blinded him to reality. At this point in his journey he was still wrestling with self and others to get what he wanted. He had a long way to go in becoming the man God desired him to be. Even after seven years his journey toward spiritual maturity had barely even begun. In many ways, his family dysfunction had only intensified. He only had dug the hole he was in even deeper.

But God had not abandoned him. In spite of Jacob's blindness and all the dysfunction it created for his new family, the Lord was still at work. God was allowing him to experience the discipline of reaping what he had sown. As Jacob pursued the path he had chosen, he learned the bitter lessons of human independence and the costliness of going it alone. Through Laban's cruel, scheming, and heartless behavior God allowed Jacob to gain a clearer picture of himself. When Jacob encountered Laban, he met his match. "A quick-tempered person may often come across another quick-tempered person. A stingy person may often come across another stingy person. A proud person may often come across another proud person. A person who likes to take advantage of others may often come across another person who equally likes to take advantage of others. These are all thorny trials. This was what Jacob was faced with at that time. God's discipline put him before a man like Laban."[22] He placed Jacob face to face "with a man more difficult, greedier, more crooked and more cunning than Jacob himself. God's plan was to let Jacob see in another person all that was hateful about himself."[23] For the first time Jacob would understand emotionally how Esau must have felt that day when he came in from hunting and discovered that Jacob had deceived his father and taken away the blessing. Through it all Jacob was feeling the grip of God. Talk about wrestling! Even in the opening and closing of his wives' wombs, God was at work overriding Jacob's blindness and opening the way through Leah's son Judah for the long-promised Messiah!

In the midst of it all "God lavished on him an unwearied but uncompromising love. Through all the shady and despicable actions that debased his life, that love was unabating, but it never tolerated or condoned his sin.[24] "Jacob have I loved," God declared (Rom. 9:13). "'Do not fear, you worm Jacob . . . ; I will help you,' declares the Lord, 'and your Redeemer is the Holy One of Israel'" (Isa. 41:14, NASB). What is weaker or more worthless than a worm? And yet that *worm* was the object of God's relentless, pursuing love. When Jacob woke up to reality, God was there!

As Madeleine L' Engle writes: "Scripture asks us to look at Jacob as he really is, to look at ourselves as we really are, and then realize that this is who God loves."[25] This is itself awesome! The apostle Paul says it so overwhelmingly wonderfully: "Once we, too, were foolish and disobedient. We were misled by others and became slaves to many wicked desires and evil pleasures. Our lives were full of evil and envy. We hated others, and they hated us. But then God our Savior showed us his kindness and love. He saved us, not because of the good things we did, but because of his mercy. He washed away our sins and gave us new life through the Holy Spirit. He generously poured out the Spirit upon us because of what Jesus Christ our Savior did. He declared us not guilty because of his great kindness. And now we know that we will inherit eternal life. These things I have told you are true" (Titus 3:3-7, NLT).

We need to lean more on God and less on our own understanding. Looking deeper than we so often do, we must see beyond the surface to the really important issues of life. And letting principle guide us rather than our feelings, our passions, or our affections, we need to climb the stairway, the ladder. There alone will we find peace and renewal—help from the Holy One of Israel.

Most of all, we need to ask ourselves some pointed questions: Am I really seeing what I think? How much do my feelings or my desires determine the direction of my life? What have I been focusing on—externals, surface things, my own plans, some person? Am I yielded to God's way? Is He as much in my focus as I am in His?

---

[1] N. J. Cohen, *Self, Struggle and Change,* p. 131.
[2] *Ibid.*
[3] *Ibid.*
[4] *Ibid.*

[5] B. Visotzky, *The Genesis of Ethics*, p. 164.

[6] *Ibid.*

[7] G. Getz, *Jacob*, p. 73.

[8] *Ibid.*, p. 78.

[9] *Ibid.*

[10] *Ibid.*

[11] *Ibid.*, pp. 78, 79.

[12] Laura Schlessinger, *How Could You Do That?! The Abdication of Character, Courage, and Conscience* (New York: HarperCollins Pub., 1996), p. 8.

[13] *Ibid.*

[14] Norman J. Cohen, p. 130.

[15] John H. Sailhamer, *The Pentateuch as Narrative* (Grand Rapids: Zondervan Pub. House, 1992), p. 197.

[16] E. G. White, *Patriarchs and Prophets*, p. 189.

[17] James Montgomery Boice, *Genesis* (Grand Rapids: Zondervan Pub House, 1985), vol. 2, p. 302.

[18] *Ibid.*, pp. 116, 117.

[19] Sailhamer, p. 195.

[20] *Ibid.*

[21] *Ibid.*

[22] W. Nee, *The God of Abraham, Isaac and Jacob*, pp. 122, 123.

[23] Theodore H. Epp, *The God of Jacob* (Lincoln, Nebr.: Back to the Bible, 1983), p. 60.

[24] J. O. Sanders, *Spiritual Manpower*, pp. 26, 27.

[25] Madeleine L'Engle, *A Stone for a Pillow* (Wheaton, Ill.: Harold Shaw Pub., 1986), p. 46.

five

MIRROR, MIRROR, ON THE WALL . . .
(Genesis 29:31–30:24)

irror, mirror, on the wall,

Who's the fairest of them all?"

As long as the queen remained youthful, the magic looking glass would always answer,

"You, O Queen, are the fairest of them all."

Since her magic mirror never lied, the queen would then breathe a sigh of relief. She was content. But as the years passed, a young maiden named Snow White quietly grew prettier and prettier, and when she was 7 years old, she was far more beautiful than the queen herself. So when the queen went to her mirror and asked if she was still the fairest in the land, the mirror answered:

"Queen, thou art of beauty rare,

But Snow White living in the glen

With seven little men

Is a thousand times more fair."

"No," the mirror replied, "Snow White is the most beautiful." It shocked and upset the queen. From that moment hatred filled her heart. It was a hatred that pervaded her days and gave her sleepless nights until she came to the place where she did everything possible to erase her rival Snow White. In the end envy literally destroyed the queen.

"Mirror, mirror, on the wall,

Who's the fairest of them all?"

I can hear Leah and Rachel each asking themselves that anxious question in the privacy of their own tent, each searching her heart and fortune in comparison to her sister and wondering: "Mirror, mirror . . . who's the fairest?" "Who's the most loved?" "Who's the more blessed?" Talk about wrestling and existential angst. The answers to those troubled questions were painfully obvious. Rachel was the stunning beauty with shapely figure and dancing bright eyes. Jacob loved her the most. To Jacob, Leah was a place to go when Rachel wasn't available. Rachel was dessert while Leah was meat and potatoes. But Leah was rich in a commodity that set women of her day on a lofty pedestal. She had sons, a troop of them.

Rachel and Leah each had something the other desperately wanted. Something they felt they just had to have in order to feel loved, worthwhile, and a complete woman. Each woman was deprived of something she most desired, tormented by what the other possessed. And each was miserable because she coveted what the other had. Neither felt whole as they endlessly compared themselves. Their fragile self-worth, burning envy, and competitive spirit ripped the happiness and peace right out of their heart and home.

Rachel said it well when she boasted over the surrogate birth of a son through her maidservant Bilhah: "With mighty wrestlings I have wrestled with my sister, *and* I have indeed prevailed" (Gen. 30:8, NASB). The word for "mighty" is *elohiym,* one of the Hebrew words for God. And the word for wrestle in this verse is *pathal,* meaning "to twist, be twisted." In other words, "with superhuman, godlike wrestling I have twisted and jerked around with my sister, and indeed I have prevailed" (paraphrase). "I have had an intense struggle with my sister, and I am winning!" (NLT).

Here we have no Disney fairy tale, but an account of envy at work in real life with real people, creating incredible pain and ever deepening family dysfunction. We could have easily predicted the devastating results of Jacob's multiple marriages to sisters. You don't have to be a marriage counselor to foresee the coming storm. It created the worst kind of favoritism, jealousy, competition, resentment, and lack of trust—all of which led to enormous unhappiness, tension, stress, anxiety, and anger.

THE COLOR THAT I AM

"Mirror, mirror, on the wall,
   Who's the fairest of them all?"

Have you ever wrestled with that one? No, you don't have a magic mirror hidden somewhere in a closet that you go to and look at and gauge yourself with. But perhaps you have stood shaving or curling your hair, and your eyes have met themselves in the bathroom mirror and you began wondering about where you were in life and how things have been going with you. Then your thoughts turn to people you know and what they are experiencing—a spouse, a sibling, a friend, a work associate—and you begin asking yourself if you are doing as well. Have what it takes. Are any good at all.

How many times have you searched your heart and compared your fortunes to those of some other person and wondered why they fared better than you? Then wished to have the same or be the same as that individual?[1] How do you feel inside when someone else is successful? Do you endure pain? wonder about yourself? compare yourself with that person? feel bad or threatened because of their success? Do you envy some other marriage, family, or person? Do you want to put people down who are more successful than you are, somehow robbing them of whatever they have attained? Do you believe that you will gain if some other person loses out or makes a mistake or moves away? Do you feel bad about yourself? That you have only half a talent or no talent at all?

The dictionary defines envy as "the feeling of discontent and ill will because of another's advantages, possession." It includes a "resentful dislike of another who has something desirable." In other words, envy is wanting what someone else has and feeling bad about yourself for not possessing it. "Envy defines 'good' as 'what I do not possess,' and hates the good that it has."[2]

Close beside envy lurks jealousy. Jealousy is the fear of losing something you already have. "When I envy, I want what you have. When I'm jealous, I'm afraid I'll lose what I already have."[3]

Both envy and jealousy grow out of a lack of self-esteem. It can happen when we don't think our needs are being met or when we're not feeling good about ourselves.[4] Perhaps it might result when we feel empty and unfulfilled because we have not developed good boundaries or taken full responsibility for our lack or for not doing something about it when we could.[5]

"Mirror, mirror, on the wall,
Who's the fairest of them all?"

Envy is a part of our everyday life. It happens in the home between children over toys, and abilities and relationships with parents. Later it occurs between marriage partners over relationships with children, some accomplishment outside the home, or some advantage or power. Envy can crop up at the workplace between colleagues and leaders. We find it in the church. All of us may envy beauty, clothes, success, financial resources, health, children, accomplishments, opportunities, pets, grades, friends, girlfriends or boyfriends. You name it! Whenever someone is more successful, luckier, richer, prettier, happier, smarter, more powerful, more interesting, can sing better, gets asked out or to do things more than you, are up front more often, it hurts.

Possessions and accomplishments are not the only things we envy. We can envy a person's character and personality as well. Someone once said that "if envy were an illness, the whole world would be a hospital." It's part of the fabric of our fallen nature and our response to the emptiness that failures and disappointments bring to our life. "Envy is probably the basest emotion we have."[6]

Let's face it, we all have envious parts to our personalities. Envy rips through family relationships with a subtly that often keeps an undercurrent of agitation and competition flowing. It can be much more devastating than the power struggles we have touched on already, because it perpetually keeps us insatiable and dissatisfied with ourselves and one another.

ALWAYS A PRICE

But nurturing envy comes with a price. When we envy, we hurt ourselves! Focusing on some other person's perceived advantages prevents us from appreciating our own unique attributes and blessings. Leah only could see Rachel and yearn to be loved like her: "Surely now my husband will love me," she told herself after the birth of her first son (Gen. 29:32, NASB). She felt tremendously insecure, jealous, and unworthy. Can you imagine a "loveless" marriage producing children left and right? Being pregnant but not kissed! "To breed he will take me. Never for love. I know the difference."[7] Each birth became an occasion to emphasize that bitterness as Leah named her newest child (verses 32-35; Gen. 30:9-13). Envy caused her to hold on to her negative feelings about herself. Remaining stuck in her bitter resentment, she succumbed to the self-perpetuating dysfunctional attitudes and actions evoked by the inequalities of her lot. Envy kept her from drawing boundaries on her feelings, attitudes, and behavior.

Rachel too was insecure, jealous, and self-depreciating. Genesis gives us enough to illuminate the dark corner of her soul that lingered despite Jacob's love and attention to her, despite her beauty, and despite Leah's constant whining about how their husband loved Rachel more. It wasn't enough. "Give me children, or else I am dead," she cries (Gen. 30:1, paraphrase). Her contemporary culture "expressed a certain heartlessness toward the childless; as the poor, the leper, and the blind are condemned to a living death, so are the barren."[8]

One modern Jewish woman who poured out her heart in a way that echoed her ancestor Rachel helps us to grasp Rachel's existential wrestling and reveals how envy could be like dry-rot in her soul. "I sit in the synagogue. The time I have dreaded is about to arrive. I am prepared, I have done all the crying beforehand. There can be few tears left. . . . I am an *akarah*—a barren woman. After three years of the latest modern tests and drugs, of artificial inseminations (using my husband's sperm), of long hours in the doctor's offices, of humiliating tests and frustrated hopes, and of moments of despair, I am still a barren woman. My husband is healthy; the problem is mine. We have used much of our savings, all of our patience. We have a serious operation to go that gives us a slight chance but may cause a serious risk to my health. . . . So I sit in the sanctuary as I hear the words . . . *P'ru ur'vu* [1.22]. God's command to be fruitful and multiply has been given again to our people. . . . [And] I feel my emptiness. As my menstrual period comes each month I mourn what could have been. . . . I feel the pain of emptiness, the despair of wanting to carry out the mitzvah [commandment] and not being able."[9]

No other love story in the entire Bible is quite like Rachel's, because "no other matriarch must contend with the pervading presence of a Leah, who is neither handmaiden nor, worse, second wife, but a first wife, sister, and exceptional among the matriarchs, bountiful mother of sons. . . . Neither beauty nor love seems to suffice. . . . Rachel wants to be not only a wife but a mother. Driven to jealousy, accusing her husband, and turning to love potions, Rachel felt unfulfilled on all three levels—as a woman, a Hebrew, and a matriarch."[10] Only through bearing children could Rachel feel whole and fulfilled. She could only see herself in light of her sister.

Envy thus unwittingly leads us to put ourselves down as we desperately try to be like the other. In the process we lose our identity. No longer ourselves, we become a clone of someone else. Furthermore, when we define our worth by someone else, by what we do, what we look like, how we are loved, or what we can accomplish, we focus outwardly rather than inwardly. We forget "being" and how God can be at work there in our inner private world. Holding on to our negative feelings about ourselves, we stay stuck in our resentment and succumb to the self-perpetuating dysfunctional attitudes and actions evoked by the inequalities of our lot. Envy can keep us from drawing boundaries on our feelings, attitudes, and behavior. We overlook matters of conscience, character, values, and motives. When we envy, we hurt ourselves!

Perhaps even worse, envy also leads us to hurt people who are around us—especially the person we envy. When Rachel saw that she could not have children, her sister's fertility so twisted her out of shape that her jealousy caused her to lash out in anger at Jacob. "Give me children or else I am dead!" (Gen. 30:1, paraphrase). Her verbal explosion threatened him. Patience had worn thin. She blamed her husband for her barrenness. Predictably, he responded with his own anger: "Am I God? . . . He is the only one able to give you children" (verse 2, NLT). It particularly frustrated him since he had been spending most of his time with Rachel (verses 15, 16). Naturally their marriage took a beating. Love turned to function, and patience and respect eroded. Communication deteriorated. Later, when Leah learned that Rachel wanted the mandrakes that her son had brought her from the field, she too lashed out at Rachel. "Wasn't it enough that you stole my husband? Now will you steal my son's mandrake roots, too?" (verse 15, NLT). Envy can make us angry, cold, judgmental, distant, critical, or gossipy. It can cause us to withdraw from the person we envy even when they are important to us, whether a spouse, a sibling, a parent.

The exchange between sisters demonstrates the extent to which envy will cause us to please ourselves and hurt others. Leah's son Reuben found some mandrake plants out in the field and brought them to his mother. Undoubtedly, she had shared her frustration with her eldest son, and wanting to help, he presented her with a plant thought to arouse sexual interest and cause fertility—a folklore love potion believed to help a woman get pregnant. Clearly, Reuben wanted his mother to be happy and to continue to win the battle over Rachel. Somehow Reuben's discovery leaked through the family grapevine back to Rachel. Chagrined and still feeling sorry for herself, Rachel begged Leah to share the plants with her (verse 14). How humiliating to beg for something you desperately want from your chief competitor! Leah, though, was so wrapped up in her own pain that she didn't seem to notice Rachel's self-demeaning behavior. She lashed out with her own hurt, further pommeling Rachel's already broken spirit. "Wasn't it enough that you stole my husband? Now will you steal my son's mandrake roots, too?" At this point Rachel found her back against the wall. She appeared beaten down. "I will let him sleep with you tonight in exchange for the mandrake roots" (verse 15, NLT). It's a very revealing statement. Though Leah seemed to have had an edge in their emotional war, Rachel obviously held the coveted sex card. She was in control of the relationship. Jacob wasn't spending time with Leah. He was not about to visit her tent without Rachel's permission, probably why Leah accused her sister of stealing her husband.

Whether or not Leah had expected such response, she wasted no time in taking action. That very evening "as Jacob was coming home from the fields, Leah went out to meet him. 'You must sleep with me tonight!' she said. 'I have paid for you with some mandrake roots my son has found.' So Jacob slept with her" (verse 16, NLT). Leah didn't ask him to be with her that night; she told him![11] In the end she literally rents Jacob for the night, paying for the attention she wanted. How do you think she felt about herself afterward? as a prostitute? We can only imagine how manipulated and frustrated and empty of love and warmth Jacob might have felt as well. When we envy, we hurt others.

Finally, envy leads us to lose our trust in God. When envy dominates our inner private world we are prone to do whatever we can to change the situation. We seek to gain the upper hand, *to fix things ourselves, our way!* Scripture tells us that beautiful Rachel was so overwhelmed by her plainer but fertile sister that she gave her personal servant Bilhah to Jacob as a surrogate mother. "Here is my slave-girl, Bilhah. Sleep with her and let her give birth on my knees; through her, then, I too shall have children!" (verse 3, New Jerusalem). Rachel envisioned Bilhah giving birth while straddling her own spread legs, perhaps pulling the baby immediately to her own body and then upward to her breasts. Symbolically the child would be hers because she had given her sexual rights to a surrogate whom she owned and who had become an extension of her own body. Though it was culturally acceptable—and even an obligation if her husband insisted—Rachel must have been at her wits' end to give her servant girl to Jacob. When Bilhah bore two sons, Rachel claimed that God was blessing her: "God has vindicated me, and has indeed heard my voice" (verse 6, NASB). In the process she revealed her heart and her motives as she cried with glee, "With mighty wrestlings I have wrestled with my sister, *and* I have indeed prevailed" (verse 8, NASB). But her "victory" was hollow and pathetic. She was wrestling in envy and passion in her own strength and scheming. Deluding herself that she had God's blessing and answered prayer. Sadly, along with polygamy, the pagan practice of surrogate mothers further eroded the moral, spiritual, and emotional balance of Rachel's inner private world.

In response Leah upped the ante by giving Jacob Zilpah, thus fighting fire with fire. How lowly must Leah have felt to have wrapped up her identity entirely in her ability to bear children to a husband who otherwise appeared to hate her? How frantic must she have been to keep an edge over her more glamorous sister that she would offer her own maidservant to her husband to match her sister's desperation?

The point is that both Leah and Rachel took things into their own hands and chose a course of action that was not only immoral, but demonstrated a lack of confidence in God. They both sought solutions that are very human (even pagan) and that caused them to lose trust in God and only created more problems for themselves. When we envy, we lose our grip on God. We take things in our own hand, and when we do, we often do the wrong kinds of things.

One can only imagine what Jacob was thinking and feeling as he found himself caught up in the envy-fueled battle between his wives. At times he may have been amused, but he must have often thought of Laban and what he had done to get him into such a mess. Sometimes he must have felt extremely lonely, manipulated, confused, and frustrated. A man in love who could never experience love the way he had envisioned it in his youth. No doubt Jacob fueled Rachel and Leah's envious wrestling with his own partiality and attitudes, his own passivity or distance. Obviously, he hadn't drawn protective boundaries in his own life and in his marriages that could have spared them much of the dysfunction. "On the other hand, it's possible that he realized more and more that the real cause of his problems were his own sinful actions that began years before in his relationship with Esau. Seeing two sisters battle it out at close range for positions of prestige and to gain attention must have served as a mirror of his own battle with Esau."[12]

GRACE, CONTENTMENT, LOVE

Our modern world teaches us to use envy to our advantage. To go after what we want—in a positive way, of course.[13] Turn your wish for harm, self-hatred, resentment, and covetousness into admiration or emulation, thought leaders tell us. Use the energy in a positive way to improve yourself. Genesis, however, calls us to lay envy fully aside and trust and wait upon the living God. The underlying message of this tragic story is that in the midst of the realities that produce dysfunctional cycles of envy, God sees, listens, and remembers. He alone can provide the blessing we so desperately seek. The context for envy was there, but Rachel and Leah could have chosen the higher ground. "Now the Lord saw that Leah was unloved, and He opened her womb" (Gen. 29:31, NASB). "God gave heed to Leah, and she conceived and bore Jacob a fifth son" (Gen. 30:17, NASB). "Then God remembered Rachel, and God gave heed to her and opened her womb" (verse 22, NASB). In the midst of this tragic story with its spiraling cycle of envy we still find God! He sees. He listens. He responds. He remembers. He gives each hurting heart a blessing—something that if received, can soothe painful wounds and break the cycle of envy. But if nurtured, envy destroys that image of God in our mind.

Genesis portrays Leah as having an ongoing relationship with God. The naming of each of her first four children is like a journal of her spiritual life and conscious decision to trust in the Lord no matter what. For her first son she chose a name that reflected her emotional pain, Reuben, "because the Lord has seen my affliction; surely my husband will love me" (Gen. 29:32, NASB). Unfortunately, her hopes of Jacob's love were dashed, but not her ability to get pregnant. So comes Simeon, "the Lord hears" (see verse 33); Levi, "there is hope for attachment" (see verse 34); and then Judah, "praise to the Lord" (see verse 35). With each birth Leah was grateful and expressed her thanksgiving to God. By the time she had given birth to her fourth son, she had come to the conclusion that she might as well give up on winning Jacob's love and attention. Perhaps she didn't want to set herself up for another disappointing experience. Consequently she turned her thoughts to heaven and simply said, "This time I will praise the Lord" (verse 35, NASB).

Only after Rachel upped the ante with a surrogate mother by giving Jacob Bilhah did Leah cave in to the moral dysfunction envy creates and try to do things in her own way. But in the end we find Leah returning to the Lord and giving Him all the credit again: "God has rewarded me. . . . God has given me good gifts for my husband. Now he will honor me, for I have given him six sons" (Gen. 30:18-20, NLT). Yes, she still battled feelings of envy. The struggle to gain Jacob's acceptance continued. Yet Leah knew God had been present in her life. Scripture affirms as much. "God can create something beautiful out of something that is ugly, sinful, and sad."[14] Woven through her painful journey were rays of sunshine that broke through the clouds that enveloped her soul. Leah experienced answers to prayer even though she lived in a loveless marriage.[15]

Only late in the story—and very briefly, at that—do we catch a glimpse of Rachel's spiritual journey and relationship with God. The Lord hasn't forgotten her. She has suffered long enough. Though He has rewarded Leah with sons because of the way she has been treated, He eventually allows Rachel to become pregnant. "Then God remembered Rachel's plight and answered her prayers by giving her a child. She became pregnant and gave birth to a son. 'God has removed my shame,' she said. And she named him Joseph, for she said, 'May the Lord give me yet another son'" (verses 22-24, NLT). One gets the impression, though, that Rachel doesn't really thank God, although she acknowledges His evident blessing. She only asks for another son. That's the play on Joseph's name: "May the Lord give me another son" (verse 24, NASB). In her moment of triumph Rachel remembers only her years of shame: "God has taken away my reproach" (verse 23, NASB). Even with a newborn in her arms—a child as beautiful as she is—that memory of her shame and her sister's triumph causes her to wish for yet one more child.

"May the Lord give me another son" (verse 24, NASB). Rachel was still not satisfied, with her beauty, with Jacob's affections, with one son. She had to catch up to Leah. But the fulfillment of her wish for another child would be her loss. The very thing she coveted the most wound up being the cause of her death. The labor of Benjamin's birth killed her. As she was dying, in those last few fleeting moments of life, Rachel named her second son Ben-oni—"the son of my sorrow."

The name expressed her bitterness, sorrow, disappointment and pain, right to the end (Gen. 35:16-18). Is it possible that the power and consequences of envy tortured beautiful Rachel to the very end? And as her life slipped away she realized without a doubt that her sister—her chief rival—would wind up with it all. Did she ever have the peace and blessing she really sought? Only God could have given her inner peace and contentment no matter what life brought her way. One cannot help wondering if Rachel pleaded with Jacob more than she did God—"Give me children or else I am dead" (Gen. 30:1, paraphrase)—ever trying to work things out on a purely human level.

Henry Varley was one of nineteenth-century England's great preachers. But "a neighboring pastor had begun to draw some members of Varley's congregation to his services because of his gift as an expositor of the Scriptures. Varley discovered that deep within him he nurtured a serious resentment toward the other man. 'I shall never forget the sense of guilt and sin that possessed me over that business. I was miserable. Was I practically saying to the Lord Jesus, "Unless the prosperity of thy church and people comes in this neighborhood by me, success had better not come"? Was I really showing ability to rejoice in another worker's service? I felt that it was sin of a very hateful character. I never asked the Lord to take away my life either before or since; but I did then, unless his grace gave me victory over this foul image of jealousy.'"[16]

"Mirror, mirror, on the wall,

Who's the fairest of them all?"

How often do you ask the question "Who's the fairest of them all?" Do you wrestle with that one?

Envy stands behind the great conflict between Christ and Satan. It dominates our fallen world. "Let us not become boastful, challenging one another, envying one another," Paul writes (Gal. 5:26, NASB). "Nothing is to be done out of jealousy or vanity; instead, out of humility of mind everyone should give preference to others, everyone pursuing not selfish interests but those of others. Make your own the mind of Christ Jesus" (Phil. 2:3-5, New Jerusalem). Think the same way Jesus did! He did not demand or cling to His rights. The only thing He coveted was our release from sin.

It takes God's transforming grace to hamstring the power of envy in our lives. Only through grace can we accept the reality that someone may have more or be more than ourselves, whether it is talents, opportunities, wisdom, friends, money, joy, or anything else. Grace alone can enable us to affirm others, to be genuinely glad with them, pray for them, help them, and speak positively about them both in public and behind their back. We need grace to be content with ourselves or our lot in life. To love without desiring all or anything that we are not. To trust that God sees, and hears, and remembers, and that He alone is the source of our blessings.

I pray that kind of grace for you. That the transforming grace of Jesus will remove envy and striving from your soul, replacing it with love and affirmation for others. Only then will you cease wrestling and be still within. "I have learned to be content whatever the circumstances," the apostle Paul wrote. "I can do everything through him who gives me strength" (Phil. 4:11, 13, NIV).

---

[1] Cilla Sheehan, *The Colors That I Am* (New York: Human Sciences Press, Inc., 1991). This children's book explains that feelings are like colors.

[2] Henry Cloud and John Townsend, *Boundaries: When to Say Yes, When to Say No to Take Control of Your Life* (Grand Rapids: Zondervan Pub. House, 1992), p. 97.

[3] Betsy Cohen, *The Snow White Syndrome* (New York: Macmillan Pub. Co., 1986), p. 23.

[4] *Ibid.*

[5] Cloud and Townsend, p. 97.

[6] *Ibid*

[7] Norma Rosen, *Biblical Women Unbound: Counter-Tales* (Philadelphia: Jewish Pub. Society, 1996), p. 82.

[8] Samuel H. Dresner, *Rachel* (Minneapolis: Fortress Press, 1994), p. 81.

[9] Blumberg, "Akara," *Shema* 17, No. 323 (Dec. 12, 1986): 1, quoted in Dresner, p. 75.

[10] Dresner, pp. 83, 84.

[11] G. Getz, *Jacob*, p. 95.

[12] *Ibid.*, p. 94.

[13] Betsy Cohen, *The Snow White Syndrome*, p. xvi.

[14] Getz, p. 99.

[15] *Ibid.*

[16] As quoted in Gordon MacDonald, *Restoring Your Spiritual Passion* (Nashville: Oliver Nelson, 1986), p. 100. See Ralph G. Turnbill, *A Minister's Obstacles* (New York: Fleming H. Revel Co., 1946), pp. 30-44, for stories and insights on the "dry-rot of covetousness" and the "bane of jealousy."

six

LIVING IN A WORLD OF LABANS

(Genesis 29:15 – 31:55)

I had left downtown San Francisco for the airport to catch a flight home. It was dark and raining, with heavy traffic on an unfamiliar route. My rental car had to be returned somewhere near the airport. And I was cutting it close.

Although I fully intended to stop and fill the gas tank, I had become preoccupied with finding my way out of the city and then figuring out which of the freeway exit options was the best for returning my car. When I finally turned onto the road where I was to check in my car—then catch a shuttle to the airport itself—I realized there were no gas stations in sight. For a moment I thought about turning around and finding one. In the interest of time, though, I said to myself, "So what if they charge me $1.75 a gallon [back in the days when a gallon of gas was only a dollar or so]? It beats driving around for another half hour looking for a gas station and then finding my way back again. I could miss my flight. I'll just let them fill it up. It's easier." So I drove on in, checked out, and . . . gulped!

They charged me $3 a gallon! Unable to believe it, I felt cheated and exploited. "This is a racket," I said to myself. "A racket that preys upon people in a hurry and unfamiliar with the area."

I had felt like that only once before in my life, when as a 14-year-old I worked on a cattle ranch. It paid me $3 a day plus room and meals to pitch manure, bail hay, mend barbed-wire fences, herd cattle, haul feed, and whatever. With 10- to 14-hour days, it was hard work from early morning till long after sunset, with no letup. I remember bailing hay in what seemed like high gear. Our employer would be on the tractor pulling a kick-baler. Attached to the baler was an enclosed wagon with seven-foot sides. Only the top was open. I would be in the wagon stacking bales. The 80- to 120-pound bales (depending on moisture content) would come flying over the top of the wagon at an unbelievable rate. By the time I placed a bale, the next bale would be just about head-height behind me. I not only needed to dodge the incoming bale, but quickly place it before the next one caught me in the back of the neck. If I got behind, it was chaos. Many times I cursed my boss under my breath, wishing he would slow down.

What really got to me was that he held back two weeks' wages. I didn't get paid until the third week I worked for him. Then it was only one week's pay that I received. He always held two weeks' pay over me. I really resented that. When I looked at all the things the man had amassed, I couldn't help wondering if it had been on the backs of little people like me. I struggled with issues of fairness and attitude a lot that summer.

Ever feel that way? Taken advantage of? Exploited? Trapped in some financial predicament or wage inequity? Some work arrangement that seems difficult or unfair and keeps you under no matter what you do?

That's how Jacob felt. Taken. Cheated. Exploited. Used. Trapped. Finally years of pent-up emotion and anger came cascading out with full fury. Jacob had just watched his father-in-law roughly turning his camp inside out. Worried that Laban would try to prevent him from leaving with all he had, Jacob had secretly slipped away with his wives, family, and flocks and headed for the land of his fathers as God had directed (Gen. 31:3). When Laban found out that Jacob had left unannounced, he was livid. To add insult to injury, he discovered his household gods missing (verse 19). Unknown to him—and to Jacob—his own daughter Rachel had stolen them. Laban's conclusion, of course, was that his son-in-law had walked off with them. So he set out in hot pursuit. A week later Laban finally overtook Jacob in the mountains of Gilead (verses 22, 23). It was an ugly confrontation.

"'What do you mean by sneaking off like this?' Laban demanded. 'Are my daughters prisoners, the plunder of war, that you have stolen them away like this? Why did you slip away secretly? I would have given you a farewell party, with joyful singing accompanied by tambourines and harps. Why didn't you let me kiss my daughters and grandchildren and tell them goodbye? You have acted very foolishly!'" (verses 26-28, NLT).

As he spoke, Laban gestured toward his many armed kinsmen, saying, "I have it in my power to do you harm" (see verse 29).

Jacob didn't flinch, though his heart likely beat faster within his chest. Laban shrugged. "I know you feel you must go, and you long intensely for your childhood home, but why have you stolen my household gods?" (verse 30, NLT).

Now Jacob understood why Laban had pursued him for seven days over hill and desert. Not for his family or to bring him his last paycheck, but for the sake of household idols manufactured from wood and clay. Jacob did not know that Rachel had stolen them, so he declared aloud for all to hear: "I rushed away because I was afraid. . . . I said to myself, 'He'll take his daughters from me by force.' But as for your household gods, let the person who has taken them die! If you find anything that belongs to you, I swear before all these relatives of ours, I will give it back without question" (verses 31, 32, NLT).

So Laban proceeded to scour the camp tent by tent. Finally he rifled through Jacob's tent and those of Leah's and Rachel's maidservants. But he found nothing. His search turned up nothing in Leah's tent. Then he examined Rachel's tent. In the meantime "Rachel had taken the household gods and had stuffed them into her camel saddle, and now she was sitting on them. So although Laban searched all the tents, he couldn't find them. 'Forgive my not getting up, Father,' Rachel explained. 'I'm having my monthly period.' So despite his thorough search, Laban didn't find them" (verses 34, 35, NLT).

That's when Jacob lost it. As he watched his father-in-law ransack his camp, he felt his fury building within him. When Laban emerged empty-handed from Rachel's tent, Jacob finally unleashed his rage at his selfish and insensitive uncle. "What is my crime?" he asked. "What is my guilt that you should hound me this way? You rummaged through all my things. Show me what you have found that belongs to you! Set it out here in front of us, before our relatives, for all to see. Let them decide who is the real owner" (verses 36, 37, paraphrase).

The outburst undoubtedly startled Laban, especially after he felt embarrassed by finding nothing. Probably he felt the fool. But Jacob was just beginning. "These twenty years I have been with you; your ewes and your female goats have not miscarried, nor have I eaten the rams of your flocks. That which was torn of beasts I did not bring to you; I bore the loss of it myself. You required it of my hand whether stolen by day or stolen by night. Thus I was: by day the heat consumed me and the frost by night, and my sleep fled from my eyes. These twenty years I have been in your house; I served you fourteen years for your two daughters, and six years for your flock, and you changed my wages ten times. If the God of my father, the God of Abraham, and the fear of Isaac, had not been for me, surely now you would have sent me away empty-handed. God has seen my affliction and the toil of my hands, so He rendered judgment last night" (verses 38-42, NASB).

Talk about wrestling! After 20 years of unfair treatment and living under suspicion, Jacob felt taken, cheated, exploited, and used. Laban was a selfish, grasping, devious, deceitful, scheming, and dishonest man. Had Jacob been at the complete mercy of Laban, he would have lost his shirt. He would have had nothing to show for all his years of work. The fact of the matter was that Laban had indeed been determined to give Jacob nothing. He was going to milk him for everything he could squeeze out of him.

Despite all of Laban's selfish exploitation, however, Genesis tells us that when Jacob left for home, he had become "exceedingly prosperous, and had large flocks and female and male servants and camels and donkeys" (Gen. 30:43, NASB). Fortunately, Jacob had an ally who was open-handed, upright, straightforward, generous, and compassionate—God!

As I read this part of Jacob's story, three seemingly unrelated themes converge in my thinking. First, the reality of how selfishness, greed, and the concern for accumulating material possessions creates incredible family dysfunction, animosity, and brokenness. Most of us have the feeling that family should be first. Our marriage should have priority. Instead, as with Laban and Jacob, we find ourselves driven or enticed or derailed by other things: material things, work, money, a better lifestyle, the "American dream." Family and relationships suffer.

Second, Jacob accumulated incredible wealth in the midst of an otherwise difficult, unfair, and exploitive situation. The economic cards were definitely stacked in Laban's favor. From a human standpoint, the father-in-law had the competitive, economic advantage. And yet it was Jacob who prospered. Why?

Third, there comes the time when the healthy thing to do is to escape or break out of some dysfunctional, abusive, or oppressive situation we find ourselves in. In other words, at times we need to draw boundaries and say, "I will no longer put up with this. I won't remain in this kind of situation any longer. I won't live this way anymore." It is only when we have drawn such boundaries that we are free to serve God fully and rejoice in His gracious blessings.

NO SIGNIFICANT DIFFERENCES

When Jacob first arrived at his uncle's house, Laban said to him, "Surely you are my bone and my flesh" (Gen. 29:14, NKJV). And Jacob stayed with him a month. After being a guest for a month, Laban said, in a seemingly polite way, "Because you are my relative, should you therefore serve me for nothing? Tell me, what should your wages be?" (verse 15, NKJV). On the surface his offer appeared gracious and generous. It was customary in his culture to entertain a visitor only three or four days before expecting him to earn his stay, but Jacob had been in Laban's home a whole month, apparently without discussion of any financial obligations. Jacob had probably been working the whole time, though. Now Laban initiated the conversation. Though his suggestion sounded benevolent, he was in reality manipulating his future son-in-law to his advantage. First, Laban was saying that Jacob's stay shouldn't be a freebie. His nephew should work and thus earn his living. Laban was only putting it in a nice way. "We're family. You shouldn't work for free. Let's strike a deal." The implication is clear: "Laban didn't want to be obligated in any way to Jacob. Furthermore, he wanted to pay Jacob a salary that would probably be comparable to what he paid a household servant. Laban was definitely maneuvering himself into a position of control."[1]

Evidently, even "before Laban raised the issue of wages, Jacob had been doing some thinking on his own."[2] When he moved into Laban's home he had quickly discovered that his uncle had two unmarried daughters, Rachel the younger and Leah the older. We can also assume that Jacob understood the local custom that a father always gave his oldest daughter in marriage first. How could he convince Laban to ignore the marriage custom so he could marry Rachel? Apparently Jacob had quickly discovered the man's materialistic interests. It wasn't hard to see at all. Only one thing dominated Laban's imagination—money! So Jacob came up with a plan that would appeal to Laban's selfishness. "I will serve you seven years for your younger daughter Rachel" (verse 18, NIV). "Jacob knew that Laban wasn't about to come out on the losing end of this deal," which "helps explain his generous offer and why he was willing to be so magnanimous with his time and energy. . . . Since Jacob loved Rachel so much, he was willing to make the personal sacrifice. In his mind, it would be well worth it!"[3]

This early exchange says volumes about Laban and Jacob. They both had business minds[4] and both looked out for number one. Each subordinated interpersonal relationships for personal advantage. Both Jacob and Laban had a way about working around cultural and family ethics in order to accomplish their agenda. Greatly concerned with life's possessions, they were the same kind of person: selfish and grasping! Laban, though, was "more difficult, greedier, more crooked and more cunning."[5] At last Jacob had met his match. It would be a long painful 20 years with Laban. Their time together would affect every family member in one way or another.

Jacob was the first to feel the squeeze when Laban slipped his eldest daughter, Leah, into his tent on his nephew's wedding night.

Although Jacob married Rachel a week later, he still had to work another seven years for her before he could receive any wages for himself. In effect, Laban not only got his firstborn daughter married off first; he received seven more years of "free" service from Jacob. But what did he create? A polygamous situation filled with incredible pain and his daughters at each other's throats over a humiliated son-in-law. Everyone watching knew the score and felt the pain—or gloated.

No one likes to lose. In the context of family it's particularly painful. When money is at the core of the win-lose dynamic, it can get downright nasty.

After 14 years with Laban, Jacob had taken about all he could, and so he asked for release from the situation sometime after Joseph's birth to Rachel. "I want to go back home," Jacob told Laban. "Let me take my wives and children, for I have earned them from you, and let me be on my way. You know I have fully paid for them with my service to you" (Gen. 30:25, 26, NLT). Jacob knew he could not just pack his bags and leave. The authority structure in his eastern extended family was complex and restrictive. To leave without Laban's permission and blessing could lead to outright war within the family clan.

"'Please don't leave me,' Laban replied, 'for I have learned by divination that the Lord has blessed me because you are here. How much do I owe you? Whatever it is, I'll pay it'" (verses 27, 28, NLT).

On the surface Laban's reaction to Jacob's request was pleasant and cordial. After all, he knew how much he had deceived and angered Jacob, who had faithfully served him. But in reality, Laban's response had as its motivation his own selfish interests. Down deep inside he was thinking only of himself. He was smart enough to realize that much of his wealth had resulted from his association with his nephew.

However, Jacob didn't trust his uncle. He responded to Laban's invitation to name his wages with caution, appealing to whatever sense of integrity and fairness might still linger in Laban's heart. "'You know how faithfully I've served you through these many years, and how your flocks and herds have grown. You had little indeed before I came, and your wealth has increased enormously. The Lord has blessed you from everything I do! But now, what about me? When should I provide for my own family?'

"'What wages do you want?' Laban asked again.

"Jacob replied, 'Don't give me anything at all. Just do one thing, and I'll go back to work for you. Let me go out among your flocks today and remove all the sheep and goats that are speckled or spotted, along with all the dark-colored sheep. Give them to me as my wages. This will make it easy for you to see whether or not I have been honest. If you find in my flock any white sheep or goats that are not speckled, you will know that I have stolen them from you'" (verses 29-33, NLT).

Jacob's lack of trust in Laban is clear. He knew he had to come up with a protective plan, one that would shield him from his father-in-law's consistent tendency to be dishonest and manipulative. Consequently, Jacob refused to accept a cash settlement or a regular salary. Rather, he proposed a "commission structure" so weighted in Laban's favor that his uncle couldn't refuse the offer. In addition, it provided a way whereby his uncle could monitor Jacob's activities.

It seemed like a good deal to Laban. But he was no dummy. While he immediately agreed to Jacob's proposal, he did so with an apparent sense of distrust. He would take no chances on Jacob's having some kind of scheme up his sleeve. Once again he took control of the situation. "That very day Laban went out and removed all the male goats that were speckled and spotted, the females that were speckled and spotted with any white patches, and all the dark-colored sheep. He placed them in the care of his sons, and they took them three days' distance from where Jacob was. Meanwhile, Jacob stayed and cared for Laban's flock" (verses 35, 36, NLT). Clearly, Laban didn't trust his nephew. It takes one to know one. He was projecting his own dishonest motives on his son-in-law. Dishonest and manipulative people often distrust others because of their own hidden agendas.[6]

Ironically, Jacob did have a secret plan! Laban's cautions did have some justification. Jacob launched a program of selective breeding whereby he carefully multiplied the spotted and streaked animals for himself. In the process he made sure he bred only strong animals for himself, leaving the weak ones for Laban (verses 37-42). Consequently, Jacob's flocks eventually became robust and highly productive. They "increased rapidly, and he became very wealthy, with many servants, camels, and donkeys" (verse 43, NLT).

His success, though, served only to increase the hostility between him and his uncle. As Jacob's flocks increased, Laban's attitude toward his son-in-law changed dramatically (Gen. 31:2). In fact, Laban frequently altered his agreement with Jacob, adjusting Jacob's wages a total of 10 times (verse 7). When Laban said the speckled animals were Jacob's, the whole flock began to produce speckled lambs. But when he changed his mind and announced that Jacob could have the streaked ones, all the lambs were born streaked (verse 8). Laban couldn't figure it out. Somehow Jacob was outsmarting him, but how? Jealousy and anger seethed inside.

It wasn't just Laban. His sons began grumbling as well. They shared their father's jealousy. "'Jacob has robbed our father!' they said. "'All his wealth has been gained at our father's expense'" (verse 1, NLT). Their malicious comments spread through the family and servant grapevine. As Jacob picked up the gossip and observed how Laban's attitude had hardened toward him, he began to get nervous. "Now he felt that he was in danger from the sons of Laban, who, looking upon his wealth as their own, might endeavor to secure it by violence. He was in great perplexity and distress, not knowing which way to turn."[7]

One more image rounds out this dysfunctional family. Jacob called Rachel and Leah into the field where he tended his flock and spoke to them in hushed tones, explaining that the Lord had summoned him back to Canaan. "As you know, I have served your father with all my might. But your father has cheated me, changing my wages time and time again. The moment has come to take what we have and get out of here. Your father is no longer friendly to me." By this time Rachel and Leah had little loyalty left for their father. "That's fine with us!" they said. "There's nothing for us here—none of our father's wealth will come to us anyway. He has reduced our rights to those of foreign women. He sold us, and what he received for us has disappeared. The riches God has given you from our father are legally ours and our children's to begin with. So go ahead and do whatever God has told you" (verses 14-16, NLT).

Selfishness, greed, and a concern for accumulating material possessions created incredible dysfunction, animosity, loss of self-worth, and brokenness in Jacob's family. It affected every member of the family in one way or another. Epp writes that "Jacob struggled to gain worldly possessions. He seemed more concerned with accumulating property than with glorifying the Lord. Although Jacob believed God and his uncle was apparently an unbeliever, it is difficult to see any differences between the two. Both were greatly concerned with the possessions of life. In our materialistic age it is also difficult to tell the difference between the believer and the unbeliever. Many Christians are so materialistic that they will make any kind of business agreement that will bring them gain."[8] Unfortunately, in the process the biggest loser is always family. Most of us have the feeling that family should be first. That our marriage should have priority. But instead, like Laban and Jacob, we find ourselves driven or enticed or derailed by other things—material things, work, money, a better lifestyle, the "American dream." And our family suffers as it feels the pinch or loss caused by greed.

PRESBYTERIAN SURPRISE

Jacob accumulated incredible wealth in the midst of an otherwise difficult, unfair, and exploitive situation. The economic cards were decidedly stacked in Laban's favor. From a human standpoint, he had the competitive, economic advantage. And yet it was Jacob who prospered. Why?

God was with Jacob in spite of his own materialistic tendencies! The Lord was with him in an economic world dominated by Laban.

Listen to Jacob's testimony:

"I see your father's attitude, that it is not friendly toward me as formerly, but the God of my father has been with me" (verse 5, NASB).

"Your father has cheated me and changed my wages ten times; however, God did not allow him to hurt me" (verse 7, NASB).

"Thus God has taken away your father's livestock and given them to me" (verse 9, NASB).

"If the God of my father, the God of Abraham, and the fear of Isaac, had not been for me, surely now you would have sent me away empty-handed. God has seen my affliction and the toil of my hands, so He rendered judgment last night" (verse 42, NASB).

Jacob knew the source of his prosperity. God's tangible blessings in the nitty-gritty financial affairs of life made the difference. Over the years those blessings built Jacob's faith and confidence in God. He mirrors how those who experience material blessings are to acknowledge that such bounties are a blessing from the Lord and not the product of their own limited abilities.

The same week in San Francisco that I mentioned at the beginning of this chapter, I joined my wife's uncle Paul and his wife, Barbara, for worship at the Community Presbyterian Church in Cambria, California, where they are members. In the middle of the service Fred Sommers, one of the group's leaders, came forward from the congregation and spoke on responsible Christian stewardship. I wondered what he might say, so I listened carefully as he spoke in a very gentle and unassuming way about the things their little church was doing, and the need for generous pledges as they put their budget together for the coming year. To my surprise, he concluded his thoughts by talking about tithe. For a few moments he outlined what tithe was and how he had not always tithed but had personally experienced God's blessings when he began doing so. He told how tithing was an expression of responsible Christian stewardship. An act of faith. A door that opened the way for God's rich blessings. You could have heard a pin drop in that little Presbyterian sanctuary. The members sat in rapt attention as this elderly member shared the biblical principle with personal conviction and thoughtful gentleness. You could feel the convicting presence of the Holy Spirit upon the hushed worshipers.

Did God just automatically, unilaterally prosper Jacob? I think not! Genesis portrays Jacob as an honest, hard-working man, someone who was self-sacrificing and industrious (verses 36-42). Even in that unpleasant, unfair, and exploitive arrangement, Jacob served Laban with all his strength and with integrity (verse 6). I believe he worked as Paul advised those of his day: "Serve wholeheartedly, as if you were serving the Lord, not men, because you know that the Lord will reward everyone for whatever good he does, whether he is slave or free" (Eph. 6:7, 8, NIV). Jacob had a good work ethic, and he didn't let the inequity of life make him bitter or cut corners. He was a hard worker, and God even blessed Laban because of him. Obviously the Lord wanted Jacob to receive proper payment for his diligent labor. He intended Jacob to have plenty, and in the process He allowed Laban to receive his share.

But Jacob's incredible wealth didn't come down to a good work ethic or an unconditional blessing from God. The patriarch also returned a faithful tithe! When God instructed him to return to Canaan, He said, "I am the God of Bethel, where you anointed a pillar, where you made a vow to Me; now arise, leave this land, and return to the land of your birth" (Gen. 31:13, NASB). Remember Jacob's vow? The one he made after he had seen the vision of the stairway? When as a fugitive dreamer he realized how awesome that wilderness place was—because God was there? "Of all that You give me I will surely give a tenth to You," Jacob had promised (Gen. 28:22). "Oh, God, since You are so graciously present with me and forgive my sins, You will be my God, and I will show my devotion in a tangible way by giving back to You a portion of all that You give me."

The Lord didn't demand the tithe. Jacob's overwhelmed heart freely promised it. God's grace led him to a consecration in tithing. Obviously, he remembered his covenant with God and as a result, God was free to bless! After years of financial hardship and abuse the Lord revealed the secret of success in a dream and worked the miracle that multiplied Jacob's efforts. The Lord gave him insight into the principles of selective breeding. But although God gave the insights, Jacob did the work. As God multiplied, Jacob prospered (Gen. 31:11, 12).

God was with the patriarch in a world dominated by Laban, and He promises to be with us in a world filled with other Labans as well. In difficult, unfair, and exploitive situations in which the economic cards are definitely stacked against us, He still stands by our side. Even when someone in our very family is giving us the pinch, God still opens windows of heaven to pour blessings upon those who trust Him by returning tithe.

"'Bring the whole tithe into the storehouse, so that there may be food in My house, and test Me now in this,' says the Lord of hosts, 'if I will not open for you the windows of heaven and pour out for you a blessing until it overflows. Then I will rebuke the devourer for you, so that it may not destroy the fruits of the ground; nor will your vine in the field cast its grapes,' says the Lord of hosts. 'All the nations will call you blessed, for you shall be a delightful land,' says the Lord of hosts" (Mal. 3:10-12, NASB).

The promise is that "God does not repay our contributions in inflated dollars or allow the benefit pool to run dry."[9] "Oh, taste and see that the Lord *is* good; blessed *is* the man *who* trusts in Him!" (Ps. 34:8, NKJV). "Test Me now in this." "Prove Me," the Lord declares. Interestingly, Malachi uses the same Hebrew words for windows of heaven that Genesis employs for the floodgates of heaven that poured out water during the Flood (Gen. 7:11; 8:2). As the floodwaters covered the earth, so will God's blessings envelop the lives of those who trust Him with their firstfruits.

In the Jacob story God emerges as the one who orders all events. He has taken sides and turned events toward His overriding promise. We observe a playful contrast in this particular episode. "The God of Jacob orders and transforms the affairs of history. By contrast, the household gods of Laban—the ones he was desperately looking for—do nothing. They must be protected"[10]— even if it is only by a menstruating woman (Gen. 31:35). Tokens of inheritance, Laban's gods cannot affect the events of real life. They are gods who can work neither good nor evil, being unable to see or hear or walk (Rev. 9:20). In contrast to the living God of heaven Laban's gods were mere objects to be carried about. The fortunes of Jacob's family depended upon the contrasting character of God and the gods.[11]

INVESTMENT HALL OF HORRORS

My third point revolves around the reality that there comes a time when the healthy thing to do is to escape or break out of some dysfunctional, abusive, or oppressive situation that we may find ourselves in. In other words, eventually we need to draw boundaries and say, "I will no longer put up with this, or remain in this kind of situation, or live this way anymore." Only then are we free to serve God fully and rejoice in His gracious blessings. Often this involves financial matters in which family spiritual equilibrium and health is at stake.

Jacob's story portrays Laban as having just one goal in mind—to keep Jacob totally dependent and enslaved. He was grasping, selfish, and controlling. As long as Jacob stayed with his father-in-law he could not be totally free to serve God fully or with integrity. Laban would always have a demand on him in a way that would put Jacob's resources constantly in question. Believers who have to live among people like Laban often face a great crisis in the faith. Do I tithe? Do I give offerings? Do I put in an honest day's work? Does God care? Does honesty pay? What about my family? my children?

Maybe it's a spouse that refuses to let us tithe or makes us feel guilty when we give a liberal offering. Perhaps it's our indebtedness or our love of money and attachment to the things of this world. There comes a time when we need to break out of the world's philosophy and attitudes of me, me, me and adopt God's attitude of give, give, give. We might follow biblical principles of finance and stewardship or just decide its time to live more simply. That it's time to cut back on trying to keep up with the Joneses. Like Jacob, we must break out of the financial dysfunction by drawing financial boundaries and being careful about our spending and accumulating. The proportion of our time and energy that we invest in gaining things versus that put on family and God must alter. We must come to grips with the stewardship of our life and means.

Revelation 18 suggests that it will be an issue God's end-time people will face when it urges, "Come out of her, my people!" (verse 4). It's a chapter about the single biggest financial meltdown that our world will ever experience. Such an event will be far greater in scope and impact than the great Black Tuesday of October 29, 1929, when the American stock market crashed unexpectedly, leaving broken dreams, shattered lives, and a global financial depression.[12]

Such a day will be more head-spinning than Meltdown Monday, October 19, 1987. That terrifying day was one of frenzied buying and selling complete with overrevved computers that flashed frantic green question marks or simply went dead and erased $1 trillion of value. Revelation's imagery is powerful: "For in one hour such great wealth has been laid waste!" (verse 17, NASB). It will be a complete financial crash for our world's final anxiety-filled generation, a generation for whom the ability to buy or sell means absolutely everything. At this defining end-time moment of human history the Lamb of God brings judgment upon a buying and selling that reflects the distorted priorities of human hearts. Babylon's destruction occurs in the midst of buying and selling. It's quick, devastating, and permanent. When that final day arrives, Revelation's Lamb stands above the financial ruins, symbolizing the true life and values that endure. It will be an epochal moment for our greed-weary planet. Wealth will have evaporated. Those caught up in its pursuit will perish. And those who survive this apocalyptic crash will have treasures that endure for eternity: eternal life, the Holy City, an earth made new, and the presence of the Lamb.

Stand back with the wide-eyed and trembling merchants who watch in horror and wrenching anguish as their financial empires and portfolios collapse before their very eyes (see verses 11-20). An examination of their lost cargo reveals a human society that sought its identity and fulfillment in material goods. Their merchandise catered to the wealthy who alone could afford such luxuries and who alone could indulge their every whim and desire. The passage's emphasis upon luxury goods reveals an indulgent value system and the greedy manipulation of the merchants who use it for their own gain. Humanity itself became a commodity in a value system that thought only of material gain and well-being. Now it's gone forever! Everything they'd ever worked for—their entire value system upon which they built their livelihood—has crumbled. Their quest for wealth leaves them only with poverty.

Where will your investments be on this apocalyptic Meltdown Monday? That's not as easy to answer as you might first think. The pithy words "Come out of her, my people" (verse 4) give the shockingly clear picture that God's own people are caught up in Babylon's hunger for more—Babylon's religion of *need!* With its Labans of the end-time, its love affair with consumption, and its preoccupation with buying and selling, Babylon operates by a distortion of values that leads to moral compromise and exploitation.

Yes, the credit cards of the remnant are run up to the max, and our homes fight over money. Our blood pressure shoots up when we're not sure how we're going to make it through another month of bills. Remnant money has gotten lost in get-rich-quick schemes and secret lottery tickets. The desire for the American dream motivates us to spend God's tithes or work on Sabbaths, or our low self-worth and helplessness drive us into compulsive buying. Which one of us wouldn't like to win the *Reader's Digest* Sweepstakes?

Tragically, many of us are more tuned into hearing the words "I can get it for you wholesale" than we are to the words of Jesus "You are bought with a price."[13] That's dangerous, because it breeds the lukewarmness that Jesus warns the Laodiceans about. Their claim that "I am rich, and have become wealthy, and have need of nothing" (Rev. 3:17, NASB) sounds dangerously close to what Babylon says to herself: "I sit as a queen and I am not a widow, and will never see mourning" (Rev. 18:7, NASB).

We must open our eyes to see that avoiding Revelation's Babylon involves more than observing the Sabbath and doctrinal purity, more than the religious moral confusion our evangelists tell us about. Babylon is about buying and selling versus worshiping the God of heaven. Buying and selling versus demonstrating our loyalty to Him by keeping His Sabbath commandment. And buying and selling versus first love for Jesus Christ. Revelation's massive use of economic and commercial language in the lament over Babylon's destruction reveals a decided secular, materialistic side to last-day Babylon. Here Revelation provides a criticism of wealth and commerce that thrusts itself ahead of obedience to God and eternal values. Tragically, Revelation tells us that God's own people get caught up in Babylon's materialistic philosophies and values. We are no different than Jacob.

You see, if we don't settle the issue of buying and selling now, we won't be prepared for the pressures coming from it in the last days. We'll be victims of the beast power, as eager to get its mark as anyone else. For years we've heard that the end-time issues will focus on the Sabbath. And they will. But Sabbath observance is an expression of stewardship, and if we don't settle issues of stewardship (which include buying and selling) now, we'll be unprepared for the life-and-death pressures of buying and selling in that day when the issue of Sabbath obedience becomes the focus. In that day, we are told, many will choose to hold on to their assets. They would rather spend their hard-earned money and keep their job than depend entirely on God's promised care, even if it involves risking their life. The absurdity comes in the fact that they will lose it all in a few months or weeks anyway, just as everybody else does.[14]

I believe the experience of Jacob's breaking away from Laban is a call to come back to the biblical principles that remind us that God owns everything. That our purpose in life is to glorify God as stewards—managers of what belongs to Him. Tithe is the minimum testimony of our Christian commitment. We should have a sense of urgency regarding our money management in light of the fast-fulfilling signs of the second coming of Jesus. Now is the time to live and use our material wealth with eternity in view. A time will come when we must consciously break with the Labans and the Laban mentality of our world so that we will be free to serve God fully and completely. We will bring our faithful tithes and generous offerings and care for the needs of the poor, affirm the priority of Christian education, support aggressive evangelism, and provide adequate buildings for ministry. As the remnant we will enter into covenant relationship in which everything we are and have is on the altar.

IN-YOUR-FACE GRACE

Can you think of any other issue we wrestle over more than this one? It's in our face because it's so much a part of our world and our life and our perception of need. The issue involves the core of our desire for security and the good life for ourselves and our families. We can't avoid it. Nor can we escape the reality of how selfishness, greed, and the concern for accumulating material possessions creates incredible family dysfunction, animosity, and brokenness—because it's all around us. While most of us sense that family should be first and our marriages have priority, we somehow instead—as did Laban and Jacob—find ourselves driven or enticed or derailed by other things. And because of it, it is *our* family and relationships that suffer.

To all of us will come the time when the healthy thing to do is to escape or break out of some dysfunctional, abusive, or oppressive situation we may find ourselves in. Only then are we free to serve God fully and rejoice in His gracious spiritual and material blessings.

Are you ready to make that radical choice? Perhaps you've already spent God's tithes or been working the Sabbath hours. Or perhaps you've compromised some business deals or not been truthful to the IRS. You feel guilty, trapped, unsure of the future. But like Jacob you can make the break and experience freedom from such bondage. Hear Revelation's summons: "Come out of her, my people." You are part of God's people. That's why He calls you just now. There is still time—time for forgiveness, to hear His promises again and let Him draw you close and renew your mind and priorities. Time still remains for you to reorient your life through His power.

A man whom I hadn't seen in church for quite a while made an appointment with me. Through all the years I had known him, he always seemed somewhat aloof. Just a "nice guy" with no deep spiritual interest or passion. It was no surprise that church attendance would not be a priority in his life. Now he was in my office telling me about the incredible things God had been doing in him. It all began with a simple prayer for a deeper relationship with God, something he had never really done before. Praying and reading Scripture was a new journey. Sometime early on God laid a burden on him about making some things right in his life. He had worked for a company for nearly 20 years and during that time he had taken various things home with him. A little part here. A tool there. He figured he had it coming to him, given the long hard hours, unfair pay, and other jerking around he'd experienced. But now God was saying, "If you really want to know Me better, make it right!" So he got out a 3 x 5 piece of paper to jot down the items he had stolen from work. Before he knew it, and to his surprise, that little slip of paper was soon full on both sides. So he transferred his list to a regular sheet of typing paper and kept remembering. By the time he had finished he had filled both sides of that sheet as well. Then came the hard part—assigning value to each item. When he finally totaled his list, it was in the thousands of dollars. Surprised beyond belief, he prayed for God to help him be a person of integrity. So he drew money out of savings and made an appointment with his employer. He would tell his story and give a check covering the full amount, with 20 percent interest.

At the meeting he got right to the point, telling how God had been speaking to him recently and had prodded him to make some things right. He detailed the thousands of dollars' worth of things he had helped himself to through the years. Then he handed his employer the check covering the company's loss plus interest, explaining that he would understand if it meant loss of employment. Through it all his employer just sat there thinking. Looking at the check. Listening. Finally he put the check in his pocket and walked out and down the hallway, leaving my friend alone and wondering how to react.

Partway down the hallway the employer turned around and came back. "What church did you say you belonged to?" he asked. About this time my friend wasn't all that excited about saying he was a Seventh-day Adventist. He didn't want to embarrass God's people or His work any more than he already had. But there was no getting around it.

"SEVENTH-DAY ADVENTIST."

"Seventh-day Adventist?" A look of surprise came over his employer's face. "You know, I have been attending a series of meetings at Andrews University [NET '98 with Dwight Nelson] and just learned about the seventh-day Sabbath. I'm trying to decide if it's for real!"

Incredible, isn't it? No wonder my friend is on fire for God now. His journey with material things took a surprising turn that ended in a powerful witness and restored spiritual passion. Talk about freedom from bondage, freedom from wrestling. And the grip of God!

Are you prepared to make that kind of radical commitment? To seek God's leading regarding principles of biblical stewardship, and then by His grace structure your life in harmony with it? "All things are ready," Ellen White tells us, "but the church is apparently upon the enchanted ground. When they shall arouse and lay their prayers, their wealth, and all their energies and resources at the feet of Jesus, the cause of truth will triumph."[15] But what will arouse us for that glorious triumph? Only when the precious words "ye are bought with a price" (1 Cor. 6:20; 7:23) overshadow any thought of our getting a better price.

---

[1] G. Getz, *Jacob*, p. 78.

[2] *Ibid.*

[3] *Ibid.*, pp. 78, 79.

[4] W. Nee, *The God of Abraham, Isaac, and Jacob*, p. 122.

[5] T. Epp, *The God of Jacob*, p. 60.

[6] *Ibid.*, p. 106.

[7] E. G. White, *Patriarchs and Prophets*, p. 193.

[8] Epp, p. 63.

[9] J. Boice, *Genesis*, p. 315.

[10] Walter Brueggemann, *Genesis* (Atlanta: John Knox Press, 1982), p. 259.

[11] *Ibid.*

[12] See Edward Robb Ellis, *A Nation in Torment: The Great American Depression 1929-1939* (New York: Coward-McCann, 1970), pp. 68-90.

[13] Eugene H. Peterson, *Reversed Thunder: The Revelation of John and the Praying Imagination* (New York: Harper San Francisco, 1988), p. 147.

[14] A number of years ago God gave Ellen White a vision of one of Satan's strategy meetings. Outlining his strategy for the last days, he counseled his angels as to the most successful plan for overcoming the faith of God's Sabbathkeeping people. "Go, make the possessors of lands and money drunk with the cares of this life. Present the world before them in its most attractive light, that they may lay up their treasure here and fix their affections upon earthly things. We must do our utmost to prevent those who labor in God's cause from obtaining the means to use against us. . . . Make them care more for money than for the upbuilding of Christ's kingdom and the spread of the truths we hate, and we need not fear their influence; for we know that every selfish, covetous person will fall under our power, and will finally be separated from God's people" (Ellen G. White, *Testimonies to Ministers and Gospel Workers* [Mountain View, Calif.: Pacific Press Pub. Assn., 1962], pp. 473, 474).

[15] Ellen G. White, *Testimonies for the Church* (Mountain View, Calif.: Pacific Press Pub. Assn., 1948), vol. 4, p. 475.

THE MAGNIFICENT DEFEAT

seven

(Genesis 32:22-31)

While browsing through the art gallery in Winter Park, Colorado, I came across another intriquing painting by Bev Dolittle titled *Night*. It was spine-tingling. The canvas was totally jet black except for the very center, where a rugged-looking frontiersman lay in his blanket. The soft amber glow of a slowly dying campfire illumined him against the vivid blackness. Only darkness lay beyond his little fire. Alarm filled his weathered face. Some chilling sound had awakened him. He was leaning on one elbow, a cocked rifle across his lap, his finger on the trigger, staring intently into the eerie blackness. The chilling anxiety of the moment was clear in his face, letting you feel the hair raised on the back of his neck as he shot up out of sleep, froze, listened, waited, searched the blackness. The man was not sure where the lurking enemy might be. Behind him? To the right? You couldn't help wondering who or what was stalking him in the darkness. The fire clearly gave away the frontiersman's position to anyone in the darkness. At a disadvantage, all he could do was wait until his stalker pounced.

It was the dead of night when Jacob worriedly moved his family across the Jabbok River (Gen. 32:22). Only one thing absorbed his thoughts—Esau. Jacob had learned that his brother was on his way with a band of 400 warriors. Esau's name is the most important word in the biblical record of this episode. It appears nine times in the 21 verses leading up to the point where we read how Jacob sent his family across the river and wound up wrestling with God—at least once in every paragraph (verses 3, 4, 6, 8, 11, 13, 17, 18, 19). At this point all Jacob could think about were his past failures and Esau's 21-year-old threat to kill him. He had waited 20 years for his mother to send him word that it was safe to return home as she had promised, but it never came (Gen. 27:41-45). It could mean only one thing. His brother hadn't cooled down yet. Then when his servants returned from their advance visit with Esau with no response except "We came to your brother Esau, and furthermore he is coming to meet you, and four hundred men are with him" (Gen. 32:6, NASB), Jacob's blood pressure shot up. He could hardly keep himself focused. Scripture tells us that he "was greatly afraid and distressed" at the alarming news of Esau's approach with his men (verse 7, NASB). It terrified Jacob. The very thought of Esau brought many a troubled foreboding and painful memory. Ellen White tells us that the reproaches of an accusing conscience made this part of his homeward journey a sad one.[1] Now that he was about to meet with Esau, his accusing conscience pricked even harder. As Shakespeare notes: "Conscience doth make cowards of us all." How could he face his brother? What was there to do? Being this close to home, closer even to Esau, things got downright scary. Jacob was no longer sure whom he could trust or what might happen, and he longed to be at peace about the things he had done. If only he could be at peace about himself, his failures, who he was. And most of all, if only he could be sure of his standing with God.

That's why Jacob prayed as he'd never done before: "O God of my grandfather Abraham and my father, Isaac—O Lord, you told me to return to my land and to my relatives, and you promised to treat me kindly. I am not worthy of all the faithfulness and unfailing love you have shown to me, your servant. When I left home, I owned nothing except a walking stick, and now my household fills two camps! O Lord, please rescue me from my brother Esau. I am afraid that he is coming to kill me, along with my wives and children. But you promised to treat me kindly and to multiply my descendants until they become as numerous as the sands along the seashore—too many to count" (verses 9-12, NLT). "I am not worthy." "You promised to treat me kindly." "O Lord, please rescue me."

Thus the night move to safeguard his family and his jittery feelings when he stayed behind alone to continue to pray in the night blackness. Jacob was in a lonely mountainous region, the haunt of wild beasts and the lurking place of robbers and murderers. Solitary and unprotected, Jacob bowed in deep distress upon the ground. It was midnight. Where was Esau? Who was watching in the darkness? Would God protect? Jacob was at a disadvantage. All he could do, really, was wait for his brother to pounce while anxiously appealing to God for help.

We can only imagine the adrenaline rush that surged through Jacob when suddenly out of the chilling blackness a strong hand gripped his shoulder (verse 24). Thinking it was an enemy, Jacob instantaneously whirled around to break free. In the darkness the two struggled for the mastery right up till first light (verse 26). It was a nightlong and exhausting wrestling match.

WRESTLING WITH ANGELS

I want us to ponder three interconnected themes in this amazing episode: The first appears in the two dimensions of Jacob's midnight wrestling match. Two encounters take place in this tale of Jacob's return home. According to the story line, Jacob is on his way to meet Esau—but he encounters God first. "On the way to *his brother,* whom he wants to appease, Jacob must deal with *his God.*"[2] It is a simple point, but it reminds us that we must deal with *where we are with God* before we can resolve *where we are with one another.* And oppositely, we cannot deal honestly with God unless we are willing to deal with one another. Jacob's story reminds us how family struggles and interpersonal struggles converge with our relationship with God. We cannot be caught up in family interpersonal conflict without it affecting our relationship with Him. Nor can we be in conflict with God without it distorting our relationships at home. Wrestling with God and wrestling with one another cannot be easily separated.

"Therefore if you are presenting your offering at the altar," Jesus said, "and there remember that your brother has something against you, leave your offering there before the altar, and go; first be reconciled to your brother, and then come and present your offering" (Matt. 5:23, 24, NASB). Here's how Blanco's *The Clear Word* puts it: "You should make things right with others before you go to worship God. And if, while you're worshiping, you remember that you have something to make right, it is better for you to leave, go and make things right and come back later, than to stay there and worship God with hatred and pride in your heart."

We find the second theme from this night of wrestling in the imagery of wrestling itself. Specifically, how the nature of wrestling positions us in relation to the person we are wrestling with. The Hebrew word *abaq* means to "wrestle," "grapple," "get dusty." I was on a wrestling team while in public school. Wrestling was a sport I tuned into regularly as a boy. I can still remember the muscular U.S. champion Bruno Samartino wearing his silver wrestling belt and strutting around the Madison Square Garden arena. And I can still feel the sparing and shoving and testing that would suddenly turn to twisting, groping, entangled bodies squirming togther on the mat. When we wrestled during recess or after school, we had no mat, only dust and grass. And when we got into real scuffles it was the same. Wrestling brings you pretty close to your opponent. In fact, you really can't get too much closer (physically, that is) than when you wrestle. Your nose gets shoved into your opponent's armpit, and you smell each other's breath. As your sweat mingles with your opponent's, bodies intertwine with an intensity that overrides any normal social etiquette of maintaining personal physical space. Both of you expend tremendous energy. And both of you share a common goal—to win.

My point is that we are closest to God when we wrestle with Him! And we are closest to others when we wrestle with them. As wrestling brings us physically close—the meshing of bodies—interpersonal wrestling brings us emotionally and psychologically close. Feelings, values, dreams, hearts, and perspectives run into one another. People we care about the most are often the very ones we wrestle with the most. It can get quite intimate. That's why it can also be so painful, intense, personal, and exhausting. The closeness of it all makes us want to avoid it most of the time. Because the experience takes too much out of us, we ignore each other or do anything possible to escape the potential for conflict. But while we may be physically distanced, the reality is that our emotions and minds are still wrestling.

Not only are we the closest to our opponents when we wrestle with them; we can also struggle with them in one of two fundamentally different ways. We can wrestle with our opponent in a dysfunctional way in which we go round and round and round contending for the supremacy, but never finding resolution, reconciliation, or understanding. For some of us, life is one long continuous dysfunctional conflict between ourselves and someone else. We're in some kind of battle all the time. Nothing really gets solved. On the other hand, we can wrestle in a way that allows a new vision of ourselves and our opponent to emerge. It enables us to achieve the kind of interpersonal breakthrough that God intends for us to experience between Him and us, or between ourselves and some other person. Every wrestling match with God, or family member, spouse, or person in our church family, has the potential for growth and a deeper closeness that was otherwise impossible without struggle.

Jacob's first reaction to a hand grasping him in the midnight blackness was to fight an assumed enemy. Was it Esau? a bandit? The patriarch determined to be no easy prey or conquest. With herculean strength Jacob struggled against what he thought was the enemy. Only as the first light of dawn began to break and God disabled his hip did he realize what was really going on—whom he was really fighting. With a new vision of his Opponent, Jacob suddenly received a new vision of himself. Now, rather than fight anymore, he yearned for closeness. In fact, he begged for a blessing from the very One he had been fighting. Sometimes we think God is the enemy. Other times we regard some other person as our enemy (and perhaps they are). But most of the time they really aren't our enemy at all. Only when we see them for who they really are can we catch a new glimpse of ourselves that will permit us to let go of our striving and desire closeness.

The book of Jeremiah provides our third theme from this night of wrestling: "We have heard a voice of trembling, of fear, and not of peace. . . . Wherefore do I see . . . all faces are turned into paleness? Alas! for that day is great, so that none is like it: it is even the time of Jacob's trouble; but he shall be saved out of it" (Jer. 30:5-7). Ellen White tells us that "Jacob's experience during that night of wrestling and anguish represents the trial through which the people of God must pass just before Christ's second coming."[3] In vision Jeremiah sees an intense period of turmoil on the horizon for the people of God in his day, and like so many of his prophecies for Israel's future, its application is in reality much broader, reaching down to the very time of the end. Jacob's night of wrestling becomes a paradigm for both Jeremiah's day and the time of the end. We are also told that "when Christ shall cease His work as mediator in man's behalf, then this time of trouble will begin. Then the case of every soul will have been decided, and there will be no atoning blood to cleanse from sin. When Jesus leaves His position as man's intercessor before God, the solemn announcement is made, 'He that is unjust, let him be unjust still: and he which is filthy, let him be filthy still: and he that is righteous, let him be righteous still: and he that is holy, let him be holy still.' Revelation 22:11. Then the restraining Spirit of God is withdrawn from the earth. As Jacob was threatened with death by his angry brother, so the people of God will be in peril from the wicked who are seeking to destroy them. And as the patriarch wrestled all night for deliverance from the hand of Esau, so the righteous will cry to God day and night for deliverance from the enemies that surround them."[4]

During that long night of wrestling Jacob's failures and sins haunted him. Satan tried to overwhelm him with guilt in order to discourage him and break his hold upon God. "Such will be the experience of God's people in the final struggle with the powers of evil. . . . Had not Jacob previously repented of his sin in obtaining the birthright by fraud, God could not have heard his prayer and mercifully preserved his life. So in the time of trouble, if the people of God had unconfessed sins to appear before them while tortured with fear and anguish, they would be overwhelmed; despair would cut off their faith, and they could not have confidence to plead with God for deliverance. But while they have a deep sense of their unworthiness, they will have no concealed wrongs to reveal. Their sins will have been blotted out by the atoning blood of Christ, and they cannot bring them to remembrance."[5]

I wonder what sins Jacob confessed during that black night of wrestling. What will be the sins that God's people confess and by Christ's atoning power gain victory over in their corresponding time of Jacob's trouble during the last days? Is it breaking the Sabbath? some lifestyle compromise? lying? impurity? No doubt such issues will haunt the imagination of God's people. But we need to remember that Jacob's existential wrestling grew out of the way he had treated his father and his brother. His wrestling at bottom revolved around the role he himself had played in his family's dysfunction and interpersonal breakdown. I believe interpersonal dynamics of family will be a major part of the turmoil that troubles the imaginations of God's people in the last days. They will be haunted by their role in dysfunctional relationships and the guilt they carry because of it.

We need to grasp the moral dimension of this coming time of Jacob's trouble, not just the doctrinal or theological parallels. Ethics will be a part of the equation of what God's people experience in the very last days. If we want to make it through Jacob's time of trouble, we need to deal with our relationship with God and the significant people around us now! In the process we will be grasping and expressing the moral vision of our unique eschatology. Ellen White tells us that "there are many who have outgrown their advent faith. They are living for the world, and while saying in their hearts, as they desire it shall be, 'My Lord delayeth His coming,' they are beating their fellow servants."[6] These are startling words. Some of God's last-day people will have "outgrown their advent faith" as if it is too naive or as if the moral values it projects no longer apply to one's behavior. They wrongly assume that they have more important things to occupy their minds with. And so they will beat their fellow servants. We cannot escape how the two are linked together—our sense of Christ's coming and how we treat those around us. Our eschatology and our ethic go hand in hand.

Jesus tells of a servant who consciously pushed his master's coming off into some blurry distant future (Matt. 24:45-51). Rather than becoming a caring person, he became abusive and mistreated his fellow servants. Here Jesus reminds us that we can never get very far from our Advent faith and remain caring people. In fact, the way we treat those around us is in proportion to how soon we sense Christ's return will be. If we ever become the "caring church" or "caring people," it will be because the hope of Christ's soon return burns with a holy passion in our hearts. As Carl Braaten writes: "Eschatology generates an ethic to go with it, or it fails to keep its promise of offering the unity of life and the possibility of total fulfilment."[7] Eschatology casts a moral vision! And so does Jacob's night of wrestling. It's typological. Paradigmatic. God's people will experience it again—you and me. Relationships are important. Our guilt and shame and dysfunction with regard to our relationships often paralyze us, keeping us from being all God wants us to be right now.

We can read Jacob's prayer of mercy and surrender in Genesis 32:9-12. Here he calls himself "unworthy of all the lovingkindness and of all the faithfulness" that God had shown him (verse 10). The Hebrew for "unworthy" (qaton) means "little" or "insignificant." "I am little," Jacob says. "Undeserving. I lack the legal credentials to make a claim for myself. I am totally dependant upon You for my welfare." His prayer begins and ends by focusing on God (verses 10, 12). Through it all he has the promise that God will deal kindly with him, and he realizes his own position of weakness. In his littleness Jacob has always stood only because of God's help.

LIMPING FORWARD

Thus far we have looked at three interconnected themes: (1) we cannot deal with God unless we are willing to deal with one another, and we cannot deal with one another unless we are willing to deal with God; (2) we can wrestle in a dysfunctional way that continues to bring pain and separation, or we can allow in the conflict a new vision of ourselves and our opponent to emerge through that will enable us to grow closer and bond; (3) these issues will be part of the equation of God's people in the very last days of earth's history. If we want to make it through Jacob's time of trouble, we need to deal with our relationship with God and those significant persons around us.

Our story ends with the image of Jacob's limping forward to meet Esau: "Now the sun rose upon him just as he crossed over Penuel, and he was limping on his thigh" (verse 31, NASB). Limping forward—it was a magnificent defeat. Jacob gained a victory and "limped every day thereafter to show others (and himself) that there are no untroubled victories" with God.[8]

"Through humiliation, repentance, and self-surrender, this sinful erring mortal prevailed with the Majesty of heaven. He had fastened his trembling grasp upon the promises of God, and the heart of Infinite Love could not turn away the sinner's plea."[9]

As the morning light began to spread across the eastern sky, God asked Jacob an incredible question: "What is your name?" (verse 27, NASB). "Jacob! The cheater. The supplanter. The deceiver—that's my name. That's who I am," the patriarch replies sadly. God forced him to confess this—then proceeded to change Jacob's name to Israel. "For you have striven with God and with men and have prevailed" (verse 28, NASB).

Jacob wins by losing, and is able to go on in the strength of the Lord. I love this picture of the limping Jacob, because it describes every one of us. And it points the way toward real victory—both personally and with family.

---

[1] E. G. White, *Patriarchs and Prophets*, p. 195.

[2] W. Brueggemann, *Genesis*, p. 267.

[3] White, *Patriarchs and Prophets*, p. 201.

[4] *Ibid.*

[5] *Ibid.*, p. 202.

[6] Ellen G. White, *Testimonies to Ministers and Gospel Workers* [Mountain View, Calif.: Pacific Press Pub. Assn., 1923], p. 77. Cf.: "The evil servant says in his heart, 'My lord delayeth His

coming.' He does not say that Christ will not come. He does not scoff at the idea of His coming. But in his heart and by his actions and words he declares that the Lord's coming is delayed. He banishes from the minds of others the conviction that the Lord is coming quickly. His influence leads men to presumptuous, careless delay. They are confirmed in their worldliness and stupor. Earthly passions, corrupt thoughts, take possession of the mind. The evil servant eats and drinks with the drunken, unites with the world in pleasure seeking. He smites his fellow servants, accusing and condemning those who are faithful to their Master. He mingles with the world. Like grows with like in transgression. It is a fearful assimilation" (Ellen G. White, *The Desire of Ages* [Mountain View, Calif.: Pacific Press Pub. Assn., 1940], p. 635).

[7] Carl E. Braaten, *Eschatology and Ethics* (Minneapolis: Augsburg Pub. House, 1974), p. 20.

[8] Brueggemann, p. 270.

[9] White, *Patriarchs and Prophets,* p. 197.

SURRENDERING ...THE GOATS

eight

(Genesis 33:1-11)

When was the last time you were afraid of someone's face? Going down a supermarket aisle, walking along some street, entering a bank lobby, or exiting through the church foyer following worship, you abruptly see someone approaching you—someone who has hurt you, or whom you have offended. Someone whom, for some reason, you don't like or don't want to be around. You are at odds with this person over something. Your personalities clash. Perhaps it's Christmas vacation, a family reunion, an occasion when you find yourself thrown into one of those important social settings, and there they are. Their face makes you freeze. Almost without thinking you turn around, drop your gaze, or go into another room. Maybe you hurriedly initiate a conversation with someone close at hand, or act as if you're busy reading a menu or program. The last thing you want is to look this person in the face. You don't want to have to deal with them—at least not now. Inwardly you're wrestling with someone you don't care to contend with, period.

We've all been there.

That's where Jacob finally found himself. On that aisle, that sidewalk, that moment at which he confronted a face that had haunted his imagination for 20 years. But he couldn't run this time. Jacob knew it was finally time to *face up* to Esau.

Face is a theme that weaves its way through the incredible episode of forgiveness and reconciliation between the alienated twins. We catch a glimpse of it in the story when we hear Jacob tell Esau, "I see your face as one sees the face of God" (Gen. 33:10, NASB). When we read the words in the context of what God later said to Jacob—when He called him to Bethel to worship Him there—we can appreciate the existential wrestling at play in this metaphor. "Then God said to Jacob, 'Arise, go up to Bethel and dwell there; and make an altar there to God, who appeared to you when you fled from the *face* of Esau your brother'" (Gen. 35:1, NKJV). Fleeing from the *"face* of Esau your brother"—his angered, vengeful, condemning, disgusted face. Esau's face haunts Jacob.

Five times just one portion of this episode uses some form of the Hebrew word for "face" *(paneh):* "'And you shall say, "Behold, your servant Jacob also is behind us."' For he said, 'I will appease him with the present that goes before me. Then afterward I will see his face; perhaps he will accept me.' So the present passed on before him, while he himself spent that night in the camp" (Gen. 32:20, 21, NASB). Jacob was in the process of sending hefty gifts for Esau on ahead with some of his servants. He had hoped the gifts would make his brother friendly so Esau would be glad to see them when they met. The play on words in these two verses is interesting: (1) the phrase "I will appease him" translates the Hebrew "I may cover his *face"* (verse 20); (2) the Hebrew "gifts that go before my *face"* is rendered "the present that goes before me" (verse 20); (3) "when I see his *face"* in the Hebrew translates pretty much just as we read: "afterward I will see his *face"* (verse 20); (4) interestingly, the Hebrew "he will raise my *face"* is rendered "he will accept me" (verse 20)—some versions translate this phrase as "forgive me" (NCV) or "receive me" (NIV); (5) finally, "so the present passed on before him" translates the Hebrew phrase "the gifts went on ahead of his *face"* (verse 21).

This theme of face highlights a Jacob who would rather die than *face* his brother. And yet, that is what he must do—including *facing* God.[1] As we have already learned, before we can deal with where we are with others we must deal with where we are with God. In the end Jacob must see the *face* of God, too. Right now, Jacob's not that certain about the outcome of either encounter.

The Genesis story line makes it very clear that Jacob's gifts—indeed the entire reunion—involve what Orientals call "face."[2] "Jacob sends a huge offering to Esau in an effort to increase Esau's *face,* for Jacob has stolen *face* from Esau back when they were children and now Jacob must offer *face* to Esau in an effort to save his own *face.*"[3] Indeed, as we have already read, "when their confrontation is over, Jacob will admit to Esau, 'Seeing your *face* was like seeing the *face* of the Lord.'... The brothers must ... reconcile *face* to *face.*"[4]

One of the hardest things in life for us to do is to look into the face of someone we are not getting along with. We don't want to see their face if they have offended us, or show our own if we've been the one to blame. As a result we don't want to be face to face with them, lest we lose any more face. Sometimes getting into a face-to-face situation with someone ends up with our losing more face. Our instinctive reaction is to want to save face or keep face as much as possible. So we turn the other way to avoid the conflict. I once read a sign that said: "Let your eyes meet His!" The level of vulnerability and intimacy that requires is more than most of us have energy for. It's even tougher to do when things are not going well—either with God or a fellow human being.

By the way, no biblical imagery better describes the existential quality of our interpersonal wrestlings than *face.* Commenting on Celtic spirituality, Irish poet and scholar John O'Donohue tells how "the human face carries mystery and is the exposure point of the mystery of the individual life. It is where the private, inner world of a person protrudes into the anonymous world. While the rest of the body is covered, the face is naked. The vulnerability of this nakedness issues a profound call for understanding and compassion. The human face is a meeting place of two unknowns: the infinity of the outer world and the unchartered, inner world to which each individual alone has access."[5] Moreover, "the human face is the subtle yet visual autobiography of each person. Regardless of how concealed or hidden the inner story of your life is, you can never successfully hide it from the world while you have a face.... The face always reveals the soul.... When you behold someone's face, you are gazing deeply into his or her life."[6] No wonder Jacob was so nervous about face-to-face encounters, with either God or Esau. Face was the window to his own loathsome and tormented soul. And he couldn't stand even to imagine what it might be like to peer through the face into the soul of one he had wronged.

MY BROTHER'S FACE

When Jacob saw Esau coming in the distance with 400 men, he immediately arranged his family into an extended column. He placed Bilhah and Zilpah and their children out front, Leah and her children next, and Rachel and Joseph last (Gen. 33:1, 2). Jacob then went on ahead to meet Esau. After his long night of wrestling, his hip throbbed with pain. As he approached his brother, Jacob painfully bowed low seven times. When Esau finally recognized his brother, he ran to meet him. As Jacob painfully raised himself off the ground that seventh time, his twin brother suddenly loomed before him, his red hair raging, his sword glinting in the sunlight. But it was Esau's open arms and tear-filled face that greeted Jacob. Esau embraced his brother affectionately and kissed him. They both burst into tears. It was a long-awaited embrace. And so good!

"Who are these people with you?" Esau finally asked as he looked up and saw Jacob's family of women and children gathering, wide-eyed with a mixture of curiosity and apprehension.

"These are the children God has graciously given to me," Jacob replied. One by one his wives and children came forward and bowed low in introduction, Rachel and Joseph presented last.

"And what were all the flocks and herds I met as I came?" Esau continued.

"They are gifts, my lord, to ensure your good will," Jacob answered.

"I have enough, my brother. Keep what you have."

"'No, please!' Jacob replied. 'If I have found favor in your eyes, accept this gift from me. For to see your face is like seeing the face of God, now that you have received me favorably'" (verse 10, NIV). "Please take my gifts, for God has been very generous to me. I have more than enough" (verse 11, NLT).

At first Esau dismissed any need for Jacob's tangible expression of reconciliation, but his brother continued to insist, so Esau finally accepted the gifts.

"While no words of actual admission of guilt are recorded the actions of the brothers speak volumes."[7] Their actions that memorable day provide some important insights for us to consider in our own interpersonal wrestling. And their respective gestures suggest steps we can follow toward reconciliation with someone we might be wrestling with.

First, Jacob's actions provide moral/spiritual imagery for those who have been the offender or the antagonist. He does two things: he sends a retinue of expensive gifts ahead to Esau, and he bows down to the ground seven times as he approaches Esau (verse 3). In effect, Jacob greets Esau as a servant or a subject would approach a king or some other dignitary—a seven-fold obeisance, submissive address, and the presentation of gifts of homage.[8]

Many feel that Jacob was merely trying to buy Esau off with expensive gifts and kowtowing. What do you think? Was Jacob back to his old tricks, purchasing favor, merely manipulating Esau by trying to pay things off? That happens, you know, a lot of times during broken relationships in the home. Something happens between Dad and Mom, or Dad and one of the kids, and rather than really dealing with the issues, Dad goes out and buys some big gift for his son or daughter, or takes Mom out shopping and purchases some expensive clothing for her. In the process the issues get ignored.

Was this what Jacob was up to? Buying favor? Smoothing things with money? I don't believe so. I believe he was letting Esau know that he was no longer any threat to his financial standing. Years ago Jacob had stolen from Esau the birthright, which included a double portion of the inheritance. But he vanished for 20 years, leaving no forwarding address. During that time Esau is rolling in the dough. In his imagination he's got it all. Now suddenly Jacob returns home. What's the first thing that would cross his brother's mind? "He's coming home for the loot! The will—he's gonna cash in on the will.

Oh, man! I'm gonna erase this guy really quick." So what does Jacob do? The twin brother, who is already incredibly wealthy on his own account—the result of God's faithful blessings and his faithful tithing—sends a retinue of expensive gifts on ahead to Esau. In so doing he's telling his twin, "I don't need your money. I'm no longer a financial threat to you. Look, Esau, you can have it all!"

As we've seen with Laban, a lot of interpersonal conflict involves protecting territory or rights or things. In fact, most interpersonal conflicts revolve around issues of rights or territory or things or status or feelings or control or sex or race or gender or money. People are afraid they will lose something or already have lost something. Jacob gives us the principle that one of the steps to reconciliation is to communicate clearly and tangibly that we want to restore our relationship with them and that we are no longer a threat to them. Jacob was interested in Esau's *face*. He wanted to appease Esau's *face* (Gen. 32:20). The Hebrew word is *kaphar,* which means "to reconcile, to cover over, make atonement, appease." It is one of the great words for atonement in the Old Testament.

Through his actions Jacob indicates his total sense of humiliation and his concern now for Esau's honor, for Esau's feelings. Jacob was guilty of all manner of things against his brother. Now he was ready at last to admit it and to do what he could to make his brother feel better—so his face would be lifted. In the process Jacob shows that there are tangible things—material as well as by way of action or words or attitudes—that we can use to express our desire for bringing reconciliation. In the process we can help lift the other person's face from one of resistance and defensiveness to one of listening and peace.

The other significant thing Jacob does is to bow seven times before Esau. That's a tough one to swallow. How would you like to bow down seven times in a row before your wife or husband, brother or sister, boss or pastor, or anyone you are in conflict with for that matter? It doesn't come easy. Jacob was expressing not only his willingness to remove all threats, but also his willingness to be a servant as well. "Hey, when I stole your birthright, I was taking charge. Now I want you to know that I'm not out to get you. I want to be your servant." That's why Jacob refers to Esau as "my lord" (Gen. 33:8).

Jacob demonstrates that there are tangible things we must do to facilitate reconciliation and rebuild relationships. It doesn't just happen. That's why Hosea declares: "Return, O Israel, to the Lord your God, for you have stumbled because of your iniquity. Take words with you and return to the Lord. Say to Him, 'Take away all iniquity and receive us graciously, that we may present the fruit of our lips'" (Hosea 14:1, 2, NASB). "For the future, repentant remnant Hosea provides the wording for a petition of forgiveness and a vow of penitence. . . . An Israelite who appeared before Yahweh was supposed to bring a sacrificial offering to guarantee his or her vow"[9] (Ex. 23:15; 34:20). Here, though, Hosea doesn't advise them to take "sacrifices." "Sacrifices are worthless without obedience"[10] (Hosea 4:8; 5:6; 6:6; 8:13). They are rather to take "words"—their confession and vow—accompanied by right action that will fulfill that promise—the fruit of their lips. To "present the fruit of our lips" "means here to fulfill the vow of repentance by good deeds."[11] It is not buying God's favor, but exhibiting genuine confession and repentance. Such responses indicate that not only do we want to be different, but choose to be so. "Actions speak louder than words" and "Talk is cheap" the old sayings remind us. The same happens with God. Here Hosea is speaking about our willingness to confess our faults and make a new start—honestly, totally, and in a way that honors our relationship with God and how we have made Him feel.

Reconciliation doesn't come automatically. We don't just all of a sudden get right with God—nor with anyone else we've blown it with. Instead, we have to take words, do tangible things such as making that phone call, writing that apology, or inviting that person to lunch. Nor does reconciliation come without personal cost or sensitivity to the feelings and person of the one whom we have offended. Each of us must "take" something with us as a tangible expression of what's going on in our heart. Even God needs to hear what we have to say, and even He desires to see what we bring as a tangible expression of our genuine desire for reconciliation.

Reconciliation requires those who have done wrong to admit it, to remove all expressions of further threat, to humble themselves, to do things that will give back their brother or sister's face—honor.

Second, Esau provides moral or spiritual imagery for those who have been offended. Has someone stomped on your toes, overrun your territory, taken something that belongs to you? How did you respond? Esau's behavior was incredible. Ellen White tells us that "while Jacob was wrestling with the Angel, another heavenly messenger was sent to Esau. In a dream, Esau beheld his brother for twenty years an exile from his father's house; he witnessed his grief at finding his mother dead; he saw him encompassed by the hosts of God."[12] In other words, in his dream Esau saw Jacob's face, and what he observed there changed his own. The midnight dream made a deep impression on Esau, helping him get into Jacob's shoes and have a feel for what his brother had been through. In his dream he saw how God had been at work in his brother's life, how Jacob felt alone, condemned, guilty, homesick, and afraid. God revealed the incredible grief that had overwhelmed Jacob when he'd heard the news that their mother had died.

Then the next morning, as the two companies finally approached each other—the desert chief leading his men of war, and Jacob and his wives and children followed by long lines of flocks and herds—Jacob limped forward, leaning upon his staff (Gen. 32:31). His recent wrestling with God had left him pale and disabled. He walked slowly and painfully, halting at every step. The sight of that crippled sufferer further softened Esau's heart and he "ran to meet him, and embraced him, and fell on his neck, and kissed him: and they wept" (Gen. 33:4). In other words, Esau took the initiative to look beyond his own hurt to that of the one who had injured him. Surprising, isn't it? We don't usually see Esau this way.

Then Esau asked Jacob about his family. "Who are these with you?" he asked (verse 5, NASB). "What do you mean by all this company which I have met?" he added (verse 8, NASB). In doing so Esau opened the way for sharing on a personal level, giving Jacob an opportunity to reveal what was on his heart. In a sense, Esau essentially implied that no apology was necessary. He didn't force his brother to say the magical words "I'm sorry"! Instead, he read between the lines of Jacob's answer about lifting his face and replied, "I have plenty, my brother; let what you have be your own" (verse 9, NASB). In other words: "It's OK! You're forgiven!"

It was a noble moment for Esau! The actions of this desert chieftain provide incredible insights into the process of reconciliation and forgiveness.

First, we need to listen to the voice of God about our interpersonal relationships, about how we feel about others or our attitudes toward them. God may give us insight into our thinking about the situation we find ourselves in as well as how the other person(s) may feel and what they are going through. Only divine intervention enables true reconciliation by establishing a spirit of listening and an openness for dialogue, compromise, forgiveness, and empathy. Esau was a man driven by feelings and emotion. Had he followed his feelings when he started out with 400 men to meet Jacob, this story would have ended differently. But he chose to receive the heavenly vision, to listen to the voice of God. To hear what God had to say about relationships rather than focus on what he felt about it. He was willing to say yes to God. I want to make the point clear that we will never be reconciled to a brother or a sister because we choose to or because we want to or because we feel like it; we will be reconciled only because we have heard the voice of God, the invitation and command of God, and have said, "OK, Lord, if that is what You want me to do, I'll do it."

Second, Esau teaches us how important it is to view our antagonist in a new way. In his dream Esau got a glimpse of a Jacob that he had never seen before. Seeing Jacob's face as a haggard and hurting one, he came to regard his brother in a new way. Perhaps for the very first time Jacob had a human face. And it called his heart out to Jacob. Like Esau, we need to view those who have hurt us in the context of their needs, struggles, and mistakes. As we see their faces we come to understand what's going on behind them, awakening compassion. The process will draw us beyond our own injuries toward their hurts and needs. More often than we realize, this kind of insight into our rival's life helps us put things into perspective, and in the process the hurt or animosity we have been holding on to suddenly doesn't seem all that important anymore.

Also Esau shows how we sometimes need to make it easy (or easier) for those who have offended us to rectify things with us. Esau didn't stop and wait for Jacob to come up with the right formula of words. Jacob was already eating humble pie with each painful bow before his approaching brother. I can imagine how with each painful bow Jacob kept asking himself, "What am I gonna say? What am I gonna say?" But Esau didn't just stand there and let his brother grovel, thinking to himself, *It's about time! Let him do seven more!* Nor did Esau wait around for Jacob to say anything. Rather, as soon as he realized who this pale crippled person was who was limping and bowing and limping and bowing, he ran to Jacob, embraced him, kissed him, and wept. Touch and tears and personal affection are important ingredients that make it easier for someone to say the things that are on their heart—most of all, "I'm sorry." Usually it is the victim who doesn't want the personal intimacy of physical closeness or contact. We instinctively keep an emotional and physical distance lest we get hurt again. Often it is the offender who will initiate or seek physical contact of some sort—a touch, an embrace—as a gesture of apology or reconciliation or comfort. But here Esau turns it around and in the process makes it easier for Jacob to say what he must.

Furthermore, like Esau, we need to receive the tangible expressions of reconciliation that someone might be offering us, whether it be an object, a kindness, a gesture, or even just words. That's something most of us find very hard to do—for example, during the footwashing service before Communion. While we don't mind washing someone else's feet, we're not all that keen about someone doing it to us. That would make us vulnerable, implying in some way that we need this person. In our interpersonal jockeying back and forth, none of us want to be a debtor or a panderer. Jacob offered Esau all kinds of gifts consciously intended to appease him. We might accuse him of manipulation. Beyond that, though, Jacob's gift-giving was an important ingredient in that it gave tangible expression to his genuine desire to lift Esau's face. Nothing lifts a face more than a gift. Genuine gifts have a way of distracting us from our antagonist's face to the place where we can sense what's in the other person's heart. For Jacob—having now wrestled with God and been changed—his gifts conveyed confession, sorrow, restitution, love, and the desire for reconciliation. Esau declined them at first, but finally received them. It was important that he did so. By accepting them he would help Jacob both express and resolve his feelings, opening the way for him to be even more personally drawn into the experience of reconciliation. Receiving gifts—tangible expressions of reconciliation—marks a decision moment deep inside where we say, "It's OK! I can be indebted to this person. I will be reconciled."

Note one more thing Esau did. He offered to go ahead of Jacob on their way back home, like a big protective motorcade.

"Well, let's be going," Esau said. "I will stay with you and lead the way."

But Jacob replied, "You can see, my lord, that some of the children are very young, and the flocks and herds have their young too. If they are driven too hard, they may die. So go on ahead of us. We will follow at our own pace and meet you at Seir."

"Well," Esau continued, "at least let me leave some of my men to guide and protect you."

"There is no reason for you to be so kind to me," Jacob insisted.

So Esau started back to Seir that same day (see verses 12-16).

Like Esau, we need to express our desire to help the very one we have wrestled with. To protect their face, as it were, and open the way for their well-being. Moving beyond the immediate moment, we must start building a solid future together by making sure the other person's welfare is assured.

"Daytime talk shows present a fantasy version of how deep-seated family rifts are healed. The alcoholic parent and abused child face off in front of an audience of millions."[13] Maybe it's the adulterous husband and wounded wife or two neighbors who have been disputing for years over property lines. "In the twelve minutes between commercial breaks, the host coaxes his guests through a cathartic cycle of recrimination and forgiveness, culminating in the obligatory tearful hug—all performed to the appreciative applause of the studio audience."[14]

Genesis offers us a more realistic view of the challenges and limitations of family and interpersonal reconciliations. It took 20 years for Jacob and Esau finally to heal the rift between them. Their story shows us that reconciliation is not a passive process. Both sides must want it and be prepared for pain. True reconciliation is a visceral experience. Jacob had to wrestle with his conscience all night, then prostrate himself in front of his brother. Esau had to come to grips with his hurt feelings and listen to the voice of God in order to be gracious and make it easier for his brother. Only after years of anguish and painful self-examination could the two brothers embrace and weep with relief in each other's arms.

SURRENDERING GOATS

I want us to catch another glimpse of that wonderful moment of reconciliation. The night before Jacob prepared a present for his brother Esau: 200 nanny goats, 20 billy goats, 200 ewes, 20 rams, 30 milk camels with their colts, 40 cows, 10 bulls, 20 female donkeys, and 10 male donkeys—more than 500 animals in all. He instructed his servants to drive them on ahead, each group of animals by itself. Then Jacob did the same with his family, sending his two wives, their children, and the closest servants ahead of him over the Jabbok. The servants went first, then Leah with her children, and finally Rachel with Joseph.

Everything was stretched out in bands across the desert toward Esau. Then, last of all, at the very back of the procession, came Jacob—all alone and limping. He had given up all to find reconciliation with Esau. All his possessions, even his family. The only thing remaining to offer was himself. And so he approached in all his weakness, bowing down seven times, calling Esau "my lord" (verse 8).

It's an incredible scene. I surrender all—all the goats, all the sheep, all the cows, all the money, my dearest possessions—but most of all I give you myself. So often we are inclined to give up this and give up that—but we cling to ourselves, and so in the end there is really no true reconciliation, only appeasement, or placation.

"Just to see your face is like seeing God's face, now that you have treated me so favorably," Jacob sobs to Esau (see verse 10). A few hours earlier, after that long night of wrestling, we heard Jacob exclaim, "I have seen God face to face, yet my life has been preserved" (Gen. 32:30, NASB). It is an incredible imagery of grace. What Jacob experienced with God he then experienced with His brother Esau—total, unmerited, compassionate grace. "In the *holy God,* there is something of the *estranged brother.* And in the *forgiving brother,* there is something of the *blessing God.* Jacob has seen the face of God. Now he knows that seeing the face of Esau is like that."[15] If God had been different, Esau would have been different. Getz captures it well when he writes: "Jacob understood as never before God's grace and forgiveness in his life. Experiencing Esau's forgiveness became a face-to-face, flesh-and-blood reminder of what God had done for him all along when he was wandering in his own wilderness of sin and disobedience. Consequently, experiencing Esau's forgiveness was 'like seeing the face of God.'"[16] God calls us to mirror the kinds of things that Esau did and in so doing know that in that kind of love and freedom of forgiveness we are showing the face of God to an estranged and hurting brother or sister. We are never more like God than when we forgive unconditionally, freely, and graciously.

Right now someone may need to see the face of God in you. Someone may need you to deal with them favorably when they don't deserve it. They require total, unmerited, compassionate grace from you—just like you yourself have received from God. "Get rid of all bitterness, rage, anger, harsh words, and slander, as well as all types of malicious behavior. Instead, be kind to each other, tenderhearted, forgiving one another, just as God through Christ has forgiven you" (Eph. 4:31, 32, NLT). "Since God chose you to be the holy people whom he loves, you must clothe yourselves with tenderhearted mercy, kindness, humility, gentleness, and patience. You must make allowance for each other's faults and forgive the person who offends you. Remember, the Lord forgave you, so you must forgive others. And the most important piece of clothing you must wear is love" (Col. 3:12-14, NLT). "Those who are peacemakers will plant seeds of peace and reap a harvest of goodness" (James 3:18, NLT). This is what it means to experience the grip of Jacob's God.

How are your interpersonal relationships? Is there some face you have trouble seeing? Are you trying to save face? Are you willing to lift the face of a brother or sister? Are you willing to surrender all? Willing to extend unmerited compassionate grace? Willing to let the welcoming face of God turn your face in welcome to someone else?

[1] V. Hamilton, *Genesis: Chapters 18-50,* p. 326.

[2] B. Visotzky, *The Genesis of Ethics,* p. 186.

[3] *Ibid.* (Italics supplied.)

[4] *Ibid.,* p. 187. (Italics supplied.)

[5] John O'Donohue, *Anam Ċara* (London: Bantam Press, 1997), pp. 66, 67.

[6] *Ibid.,* p. 63.

[7] Stuart Briscoe, *Genesis* (Dallas: Word Pub., 1987), p. 280.

[8] Claus Westermann, *Genesis 12-36* (Minneapolis: Augsburg Pub. House, 1985), p. 524.

[9] Douglas Stuart, *Hosea-Jonah, Word Biblical Commentary* (Waco, Tex.: Word Books, 1987), vol. 31, p. 213.

[10] *Ibid.*

[11] *Ibid.*

[12] E. G. White, *Patriarchs and Prophets,* p. 198.

[13] N. Rosenblatt and J. Horwitz, *Wrestling With Angels,* p. 302.

[14] *Ibid.*

[15] W. Brueggemann, *Genesis,* pp. 272, 273.

[16] G. Getz, *Jacob,* p. 157.

THE RAPE OF DINAH

nine

(Genesis 33:18 – 34:31)

Dinah was a young girl, curious about the customs and the dress of the local women who lived within the walled city near the place where her family had pitched camp. The young prince of the city, Shechem son of Hamor the Hivite, noticed Dinah strolling through his streets and decided to have his way with her. When her father didn't seem to do anything about it, Dinah's brothers took matters into their own hands. An R-rated episode filled with lust, rape, humiliation, pillage, greed, and bloody revenge, it was quite an interruption in Jacob's journey home with his family and possessions. Most of our Sabbath school teachers delete it from our Bible study, and it's the kind of story you either read in a hurry or skip over. But Scripture is not afraid to touch on such things. The Bible would have us grapple with the complex ethical issues it raises for families, because it reminds us what can happen when first things aren't really first in our homes.

SPIRITUAL VERTIGO

On the evening of July 16, 1999, John F. Kennedy, Jr., his wife, Carolyn, and her sister, Lauren Bessette, were scheduled to arrive in Martha's Vineyard, Massachusetts, for a family wedding. But they never made it. Instead the high-performance single-engine Piper Saratoga they were flying mysteriously plunged out of the sky into the dark Atlantic waters.

Nearly a year after Kennedy plummeted into the sea, the

National Transportation Safety Board confirmed preliminary reports and suspicions held since the crash—that the son of the late president had become disoriented in the night sky and lost control of the aircraft. The wording in the report blamed the crash on "spatial disorientation" or vertigo. Spacial disorientation is confusion in the brain that results from a loss of balance in the inner ear, creating an inability to determine accurately the attitude or motion of the aircraft in relation to the earth's surface. Pilots think they are level when in fact they are turning or plunging. At night or in cloudy skies the brain has few visual landmarks to orient itself. The inability to perceive the natural horizon or surface references is common during flights over water, at night, in sparsely populated areas, and in low visibility—all situations true for Kennedy. The inky skies, the dark ocean, the midsummer haze, and the lack of landmarks were a deadly combination. A pilot not trained to use flight instruments (as Kennedy wasn't) can begin a dive—even a steep one—without realizing it. You literally lose control of the plane, and you can't determine if you're climbing, descending, turning, or flying level. It explains the erratic movements recorded by radar and how within a span of just a few seconds Kennedy's plane plunged 5,000 feet per minute, 10 times the normal rate, in an apparent "graveyard spiral" and out of control.[1]

When Jacob pitched his tent outside the city of Shechem, he and his family experienced spiritual vertigo. They encountered powerful social forces and cultural values that fundamentally altered their moral and ethical sense of what was, in fact, right and wrong. Camping outside the city of Shechem, they became disoriented. Their moral compass was thrown off, and they didn't even know it. They began a downward moral-spiritual "graveyard spiral" that threatened to destroy their family and their very identity as God's people.

Scripture tells us that Jacob pitched his tent before the city (Gen. 33:18). Interestingly, the Hebrew word for "city" is *îr*, which can also be translated "excitement, rouse oneself, awake, incite."[2] This Hebrew word appears in the fourth chapter of Genesis, in which Cain, running from God, builds the first city (verse 17). It occurs again in chapter 11, in which humanity builds the Tower of Babel as part of the spirit of a great booming city (Gen. 11:4, 5, 8). Cain and his descendants worked hard to make the world a safe place by building cities, developing agriculture, producing music and works of art (Gen. 4:17-22). Their response to the divine curse was to make life easy, civilized, enjoyable, entertaining, and safe. They placed value on womanhood and external beauty as well as pride and boasting of power and self-assertion.[3] As Jacques Ellul writes: "The life of a powerful city is but a constant succession of revolts against God."[4] Education, culture, art, and work so often take the place of God in our lives. They provide a sense of fulfillment and identity, but it is only a mirage. Revolt against God was part of the city at Babel as well: "Then they said, 'Come, let us build ourselves a city, and a tower with its top in the heavens, and let us make a name for ourselves; otherwise we shall be scattered abroad upon the face of the whole earth.' The Lord came down to see the city and the tower, which mortals had built. And the Lord said, 'Look, they are one people, and they have all one language; and this is only the beginning of what they will do; nothing that they propose to do will now be impossible for them. Come, let us go down, and confuse their language there, so that they will not understand one another's speech.' So the Lord scattered them abroad from there over the face of all the earth, and they left off building the city" (Gen. 11:4-8, NRSV).

My point is that Genesis links the appearance of civilization and art in human history to human self-assertion and rebellion against God. When men or women face spiritual emptiness they work hard to become powerful, to keep the absence of God in their lives from having its effects. They create the arts and sciences, raise armies, and build cities. Human beings respond to the divine curse with the spirit of might. I'm making a judgment, not about music, arts, aesthetics, culture, or technology, but about the spiritual and moral context from which these cultural realities (and their moral-spiritual perspectives) so often develop. There's nothing intrinsically wrong with art, beauty, artisanship, music, culture, or city. Scripture presents each of these realities in very positive and wholesome contexts as well. However, there can be something wrong with the energy and motive that fuel them. They can convey and mirror restlessness, anger, disillusionment, and hopelessness. The biblical notion of city outside the sphere of God's sovereign presence captures it well.

Scripture does not tie culture and sin together in such a way as to make one dependent on the other, but by placing them side by side (Gen. 4; Gen. 11; Rev. 18, etc.) it shows at what length the restless human heart will reach to in order find hope and peace and security and blessing. Furthermore, as the Hebrew word for city implies, cities by nature have a drawing power that engages human curiosity and elicits participation. Someone has said that "night breeds its own sort of anticipation." We could make the same claim of city.

Shechem was an ancient Canaanite religious center.[5] Like many cities of the world, it was a cultural power that disseminated its worldview in a myriad of enchanting and tangible ways. When Jacob settled in Shechem, he unwittingly subjected his family to an extremely worldly environment. That's the point of this tragic story. Interestingly, Scripture tells us that Jacob set up an altar and worshiped God there outside Shechem's walls (Gen. 33:20). The paradox of this passage, though, is that while Jacob worships God, this city and all that it stood for in terms of contemporary culture and the values it disseminated through its customs, products, and ethos was drowning out his worship. Which do you think had the stronger pull on this family's imagination? The ho-hum rut of morning and evening worship—Dad's religion—or the magnetic attraction of the city? The few moments of worship, or the incessant throb of an exciting city? It reminds us that we can float along lifelessly and lukewarm as Christian families—faithfully worshiping from day to day and Sabbath to Sabbath—but the real influence in our lives comes from our living smack-dab in the world and all that it offers.

Jacob obviously miscalculated the impact his decision to reside near Shechem would have on his family. As a result, "he paid a terrible price when Dinah fell prey" to its prince.[6] It is true that we cannot remove ourselves from the world's systems or retreat as hermits. Nor can we ever completely escape the subtle molding influence of culture around us. We have no choice but to live in the world. But we must make every effort not to become part of it. "I'm not asking you to take them out of the world, but to keep them safe from the evil one," Jesus prayed (John 17:15, NLT). Being in the world but not of the world involves our heart orientation and values. "Stop loving this evil world and all that it offers you, for when you love the world, you show that you do not have the love of the Father in you. For the world offers only the lust for physical pleasure, the lust for everything we see, and pride in our possessions. These are not from the Father. They are from this evil world" (1 John 2:15, 16, NLT). Too many Christian families settle in places that will give them worldly advantage without considering the proper environment of home, church, school and God's place of service for them. I'm not talking only about location, but how we face the world and open ourselves to it via the avenues through which it presents itself to us: TV, technology, Internet, arts, etc.

Some suggest that when Jacob halted at Shechem and purchased a piece of land he stopped short of fully following God's instructions. The Lord had told him to return to his homeland, the land of his fathers and his relatives. "I am the God *of* Bethel, where you anointed a pillar, where you made a vow to Me; now arise, leave this land, and return to the land of your birth" (Gen. 31:13, NASB). Jacob was to journey as far as Mamre of Kiriatharba (Hebron), where his grandfather Abraham had lived and where his father awaited his return (Gen. 35:27; 37:1). But he stopped short even of Bethel and decided to settled in Shechem. At best it was only partial obedience.[7] Maybe he reasoned that he was at least across the border and in Canaan. Perhaps the grazing was good near Shechem. Evidently Jacob was seeking earthly advantages. At one point along the way he had even stopped to build himself a house, including shelters for his livestock (Gen. 33:17), thus temporarily abandoning his tent. There was nothing sinful about building a house or having earthly advantage or possessions. The problem lay in that he had not completely followed God's instructions. Shechem was farther along, but still short of where God wanted him to settle. "Jacob did not completely obey God, and he began to reap what he had sown, particularly in the lives of his children, for whose advantages he had probably settled in Shechem. One cannot stop short of God's will, purpose and place of service without reaping some bad fruit."[8]

If this interpretation of Jacob's movements is valid, then through Dinah's rape Jacob began "reaping the results of incomplete obedience as well.... What a heartbreaking experience this must have been for Jacob."[9] Because Jacob obeyed only partially, because he wasn't careful about where he was, he created the situation in which his only daughter would be tempted to investigate the world around her.

As a parent, it is hard to read something like this without feeling a bit guilty. "How have I pitched my family tent before Shechem? What kinds of things have I been unwittingly exposing my children to through my priorities and decisions? What am I doing that renders my children morally and spiritually vulnerable? Do I think about it that much?" While in a shopping mall I noticed a large character education display of what looked like gelatin with all kinds of fruit and stuff suspended in its congealed hold. The advertisement stated that a young person's brain is like Jell-O and encouraged parents to be sure that they get the right values inserted into their son or daughter's mind before their moral spiritual thinking jells for good. That's what this episode in Jacob's life is all about—not only how city forms the moral imagination of our young people, but how we often bring city right into our home, thus rendering our young people vulnerable to popular culture.

LIKE MOTHER, LIKE DAUGHTER?

A parent's own example or lack of presence in a young person's life can also create the setting for spiritual vertigo. The rabbis hold Dinah partly to blame for her rape while at Shechem. And they place some responsibility on Leah for her daughter's tragic experience as well.[10] They take their cue from the opening words of the story: "Now Dinah, the daughter of Leah . . . went out to visit the daughters of the land" (Gen. 34:1, NASB), suggesting that the verbal form "went out," instead of the more common "went," implies that Dinah was gadding about, looking for trouble. The rabbis also feel that the phrase "the daughter of Leah," instead of "daughter of Jacob," hints that in this respect Dinah acted like her mother.[11]

The Hebrew word "went out," then, is the key. Remember the mandrakes, the folklore love potion that Leah and Rachel haggled over? Rachel got the mandrakes because she agreed to let Leah sleep with Jacob that night. Rachel held the "sex card" in the family. Finally Leah had intimate access to Jacob. Even if it were for one night, her track record of being fertile was on her side. And she didn't waste any time. Scripture tells us that "when Jacob came in from the fields that evening, Leah went out to meet him. 'You must sleep with me,' she said. 'I have hired you with my son's mandrakes.' So he slept with her that night" (Gen. 30:16, NIV).

Do you think Leah *went out* to meet Jacob looking like a hag and smelling like a dog? Did she wear 12 layers of the most modest and matronly looking clothing she could find? Do you believe she spoke to her husband in a gruff, commanding voice or a demeaning tone? No! Leah was the "incubator" who longed to be loved. She may have been a bit crude about what she said and did that day, but I imagine she was decked out, dressed as attractively and as seductively as she could be, and perfumed to the hilt. Sexy is the word. In fact, you can read a bit of erotic foreplay in her words, "You must sleep with me tonight. . . . I have hired you." If, as some suggest, the largest human sex organ is the brain, Leah knew what she was doing when she went out to stir Jacob's imagination and make the evening together memorable.

The way the rabbis read it: "As the one *went out* immodestly, so did the other. Dinah was a *yatzanit* [gadabout] just like Leah."[12] So as Ezekiel puts it: "Everyone who quotes proverbs will quote this proverb about you: 'Like mother, like daughter'" (Eze. 16:44, NIV). But wait a minute! Can one always tell the immorality of the mother from the daughter? Let's get some perspective here.

First, Leah was no slut. If she prettied herself and went out to Jacob wearing suggestive clothing and whispering provocative words, she did so as a wife longing for intimacy beyond sex. But sex does get a man's attention. And suggestive female behavior in any form—whether involving clothing, words, demeanor, or eyes—turns many a male eye. Leah did not proposition Jacob behind drawn tent flaps. She *went out* to him in broad daylight. Dinah (and the rest of the kids) likely saw the whole thing. The fact that it was one of the young people in the family who brought the mandrakes home in the first place suggests a natural interest about sex in Jacob's home. So, like any young person curious about their sexuality, Dinah likely learned a lesson from Mom that day that unwittingly inclined her toward sensuality—perhaps in words, dress, and demeanor. What Leah did for a worthy purpose, Dinah may have done for an unworthy one.[13]

Is it possible that Shechem's rape of Dinah, Reuben's interest in mandrakes, his bedding of one of Leah's maidservants—Jacob's concubine (Gen. 35:22)—and Judah's afternoon romp with a prostitute (his daughter-in-law, Tamar [Gen. 38:1-19]) betray a bit of the sex-saturated culture emanating from Shechem? I think so. Perhaps Dinah was only playing a game—a kind of "look but don't touch" —that Shechem wasn't about to honor. Some of the blame for these moral lapses could lie squarely on parental example.

Again, as a parent it is hard to read something like this without asking yourself some tough questions. "How have my actions, my choices, or my attitudes—my way of seeing and doing things—influenced the manner in which a young person in my home might view their world, their sexuality, their sense of identity, their behaviors and attitudes?"

DADDY'S LITTLE GIRL?

Jonetta Rose Barras has written a book called *Whatever Happened to Daddy's Little Girl?* in which she discusses the devastating impact of fatherlessness on Black women. Desperately seeking love, fatherless women often feel abandoned, unworthy, and empty. They often fill the void in ways that only make the hole larger and deeper. Barras writes that young women whose fathers may be physically present but "emotionally unavailable" may also express many of the symptoms of the fatherless woman syndrome. These include: feeling unworthy and unlovable; fear of rejection, abandonment, and commitment; sexual expression ranging from promiscuity to an aversion to intimacy; the need to overcompensate, overachieve, or oversaturate; and rage, anger, and depression.[14]

Norman Wright's *Always Daddy's Girl: Understanding Your Father's Impact on Who You Are* posits similar conclusions. He notes that a dysfunctional family is one that has strayed off course. "In most cases, a dysfunctional family is the product of a dysfunctional husband-father, one who failed to occupy a healthy, positive role due to uninvolvement, domination, illness/death, desertion/divorce, etc."[15] Unfortunately, the product of a dysfunctional husband-father in the home is often more apparent in the life of the father's daughter(s) than in any other relationship. Instead of recalling tender memories of the first significant man in their life, many women look back and see only empty arms and unspoken words of love and acceptance. Their relationship with their father has significant impact on shaping their identity and behavior.

Dinah was a young girl, curious about the customs and the dress of the local women who lived in Shechem. Is it possible that the reality that Jacob didn't distribute his affections evenly between his wives and their children helped fuel that interest? That he had favorites and had been emotionally stingy with Leah's sons and daughter? Perhaps that is why Simeon and Levi—Dinah's two brothers through Leah—are the ones who step forward to rescue her (Gen. 34:25, 30, 31). They didn't think Dad cared enough or would do anything about it. I think so! It makes us wonder how we may be withholding emotional support from some young person in our life or how our "emotional unavailability" is playing out in our sons' and daughters' lives. It's both a father and a mother thing.

WHO WILL BECOME LIKE THE OTHER?

Surprisingly, after he raped Dinah, Shechem became captivated by her. Since that's not usually the case, there must have been something about Dinah that was bewitching beyond her physical conquest. He fell in love with her and tried to win her heart by speaking tenderly to her (verse 3). Were they words of apology? sorrow? We don't know. But he wanted to woo her. And to his father, Hamor, he announced, "Get me this girl; I want to marry her."

Meanwhile, Jacob somehow heard how his daughter Dinah had been dishonored, but did not know how to respond. "Having just moved to this region, he wasn't eager to pick a fight with a much more powerful and established adversary who occupied a fortified city. How could he recover his daughter without putting his entire tribe at risk? He decided to do nothing until he could confer with his sons."[16] Since his sons were out in the countryside with his livestock, Jacob decided to remain silent until they returned (verse 5).

In the meantime Hamor came out to discuss the matter with Jacob (verse 6). Hamor had recently done business with Jacob, selling him the site for his tents for 100 pieces of silver (Gen. 33:18, 19). He evidently thought it best to deal directly with Jacob in order to placate Dinah's family for the grievous offense his son had committed.

Jacob's sons heard the news when they came in from the field at the close of the day. Shocked and furious that their sister had been raped, they erupted instantly (Gen. 34:7). In their opinion Shechem's action was a *nebalah*—a folly and disgrace. The Hebrew word used is an angry one "referring to serious violation of the community" (Joshua 7:15; Judges 19:23ff.; 2 Sam. 13:12).[17] It was "a disgraceful thing [done] against Jacob's family" (Gen. 34:7, NLT). Their response shows that the violation of their sister went against their moral values and was unacceptable.

Hamor could read the looks on their faces and got right to the point. "My son Shechem is truly in love with your daughter, and he longs for her to be his wife. Please let him marry her. We invite you to let your daughters marry our sons, and we will give our daughters as wives for your young men. And you may live among us; the land is open to you! Settle here and trade with us. You are free to acquire property among us" (verses 8-10, NLT). Obviously the Shechemite ruler believed that he was making a generous offer. How could "nomads not be pacified by his invitation to become citizens of Shechem? They would prosper, and the town would certainly benefit from the addition of this industrious tribe. Best of all, his son would acquire a woman whom he loved."[18]

Then Shechem, who had come out with his father to meet Dinah's family, now spoke on his own accord: "'Please be kind to me, and let me have her as my wife,' he begged. 'I will give whatever you require. No matter what dowry or gift you demand, I will pay it—only give me the girl as my wife'" (verses 11, 12, NLT).

Jacob's sons weren't so sure about this, so they offered a counterproposal. They demanded that Hamor and Shechem's people make themselves *qualified* to participate in the Hebrew community by agreeing to circumcise all their males. Only then could they become one community, and marriage would thus be an open matter (verses 14-17). If the men of Shechem would not agree to be circumcised, then Dinah's family would take her and be on their way. Scripture informs us that they were bluffing in their counterproposal (verse 13). Evidently, they purposefully set a bride price that they figured Shechem and the other men of the city would have to refuse.[19] What adult male would want to go through that kind of pain and humiliation? And for what? After all, the prince still held Dinah within the city (verse 26), so the brothers were not really negotiating from a position of strength.

Surprisingly, it sounded like a good idea to Hamor and Shechem. So the king and his son went back to the gate of the city and spoke with the men of Shechem. "'Those men are our friends,' they said. 'Let's invite them to live here among us and ply their trade. For the land is large enough to hold them, and we can intermarry with them. But they will consider staying here only on one condition. Every one of us men must be circumcised, just as they are. But if we do this, all their flocks and possessions will become ours. Come, let's agree to this so they will settle here among us.' So all the men agreed and were circumcised" (verses 21-24, NLT).

A theme runs through this story. Hamor speaks to Jacob of an intermarriage of the two communities that would bring material possessions, property, and financial advantage for the patriarch and his family. Later Jacob's sons essentially say, "If you become like us [being circumcised] we'll become one with you." Finally, Hamor persuades the men of Shechem to be circumcised with the promise that intermarriage would enable them to acquire the cattle, possessions, and all the animals of Jacob's family. So delighted were the townsmen by the prospect of getting Jacob's flocks that they barely flinched at the terms. A few days of humiliation and pain would be worth the gain.

The question in the narrative comes down to who will become like the other. Will the people of God become one with the world or will the world become one with the people of God? How much and in what way will one become like the other? And who stands to gain the most in the proposed arrangement? The story's plot points both to the powerful integrating nature of culture and to the issue of identity on the part of God's people. As Naomi Rosenblatt and Joshua Horwitz write: "Jacob and his sons were in a precarious position. They had been invited to join the people of Shechem, and they knew if they intermarried they would soon be absorbed into an alien people and face extinction."[20]

Who would become like the other? That's the fundamental question that every generation of God's people faces in relation to the world. It is the question every God-fearing family encounters relative to the seducing power of popular culture. Pitching our tent before the city creates tremendous pressure and forces the issue of identity. Interestingly, the incident demonstrates that "even unbelievers will compromise and agree to religious vows if they think they will profit."[21]

WHEN PARENTS FAIL TO LEAD

Three days after being circumcised, the men of Shechem were in great pain and quite vulnerable. During that defenseless moment "two of Dinah's brothers, Simeon and Levi, took their swords, entered the town without opposition, and slaughtered every man there, including Hamor and Shechem. They rescued Dinah from Shechem's house and returned to their camp. Then all of Jacob's sons plundered the town because their sister had been defiled there. They seized all the flocks and herds and donkeys—everything they could lay their hands on, both inside the town and outside in the fields. They also took all the women and children and wealth of every kind" (verses 25-29, NLT).

Surprisingly, Jacob's response to his son's violent retribution seems more concerned with survival than with ethical behavior: "Afterward Jacob said to Levi and Simeon, 'You have made me stink among all the people of this land—among all the Canaanites and Perizzites. We are so few that they will come and crush us. We will all be killed!'" (verse 30, NLT). The patriarch did not rebuke them for their morality, but rather for the fact that their behavior put the whole family in danger. He did not speak of the sin and dishonor their actions had been to God. All that Jacob seemed to be concerned about was what people would do to him. According to the story, Shechem was an important urban prince and the family of Jacob mere part-time farmers and herders.[22]

But Jacob's sons stood their ground: "Should our sister be made a whore?" (see verse 31). They must have doubted that Jacob would go to any great trouble to rescue Dinah. After all, Dad had never been in love with their mother. He likely didn't show them the attention they yearned for either. If he was as emotionally detached as they felt he was, why would he be interested in their welfare? So they'd stick up for themselves, their honor, their dignity, their sister.

Rosenblatt and Horwitz note that "beneath this tragedy lies a strong indictment of parents who forfeit their moral authority as family leaders. Hamor, for one, doesn't seem the least bit concerned that his son has raped a girl and held her captive. He treats the whole incident as an everyday exercise of his private and public power"[23]—money talks, and so do a few diplomatic words. As for Jacob, he assumes a decidedly passive role in resolving the family crisis. The patriarch "knows he has distributed his affections unevenly between his two wives. . . . Jacob has probably been emotionally stingy with [Leah's] sons and daughter. Now, when Dinah is raped and held captive, Jacob is paralyzed."[24] As a father he doesn't seem to have the moral authority he needs to lead. So "Dinah's brothers step forward into the vacuum left by their father's inertia. . . . When our children feel wronged, they vent their rage in all directions with little concern for proportion or consequence."[25]

Through it all Dinah becomes a nonperson in the story as she "plays no role in it after the opening verse. She becomes a nonperson in the drama,"[26] and the biblical narrative never mentions her again. We read only of all the men in her life trying to solve the problem. Consequently, we can assume that her rape robbed her of a future. The tragic reality of rape and other forms of sexual victimization has not materially changed through the millennia. Those abused become nonpersons unable to speak or act for themselves.

The rape of Dinah is a story that ends without resolution, without any common ground between Jacob and his sons, and with Dinah as a nonperson. "In this story no relationship is resolved, none reconciled."[27] Instead, we find only alienation, loneliness, fear, and pain. Talk about wrestling! The incident depicts hurting parents, children, and community.

HITTING BOTTOM

The lesson that stands out in this tragic incident is the impact of unthoughtfully mingling with contemporary culture—with the world. It points to the spiritual-moral impact culture has on our lives and how the larger world around us and its spiritual-moral values affect family. The dynamics of our larger world intrude on family peace, sometimes bringing out the very worst. The story of Jacob's family at Shechem illustrates how our world draws us out to itself, crushes us, spreads pain through our family, tries to make us like itself by encapsulating us in its value system—even as we continue to worship God. The rape of Dinah is a commentary on how parents can unwittingly create a context for young people to become vulnerable to the world's influence, even cause them to vent their anger and feelings in ways that bring even more pain.

Jacob's children experienced the tragic effects of his unfaithfulness. Furthermore, their father could have no testimony among the people where he lived because of his compromise and worldliness.[28]

"Worldliness completely overwhelmed him. He could not have gone any lower, and his family could not have gone any lower. Their reputation among the people around them was destroyed."[29] As a family, they had veered off course with spiraling dysfunction and resulting pain.

No parent can read this story without struggling with existential questions: "How have I pitched my family tent before Shechem? What kinds of things have I been exposing them to through my priorities and decisions? How have my actions, my choices, or my attitudes—my way of seeing and doing things—influenced the manner in which a young person in my home might view their world, their sexuality, their sense of identity, their behaviors and attitudes? How have I withheld emotional support from some young person in my home? Could it be that surprise child I never wanted or that forced me into marriage? My spouse's child in our blended family? That young person who reminds me so much of someone I don't like? Finally, who is becoming like whom? Are I and my family becoming encapsulated into the culture around us? Or are we still distinct, decidedly Christian, salt in the earth?

Stephen Covey suggests that "one of the worst feelings in the world is when you realize that the 'first things' in your life—including family—are getting pushed into second or third place, or even further down the list. And it becomes even worse when you realize what's happening as a result."[30] The rape of Dinah and the slaughter of the men, women, and children of Shechem undoubtedly stand out as one of the worst moments of Jacob's life. Many of us can identify with his experience. We intuitively trace the pain in our family to our ourselves—our failures—and it doesn't feel too good.

The key to resisting the molding influence of culture is to become aware of the pernicious, sinister impact it has on our family's moral imagination, values, and behavior. The rape of Dinah and its aftermath create just such a moment for reflection. Many parents find themselves in anguish of soul because of the worldliness of their children. Here's a story that points to reasons why that may be so. It can direct us to the positive values needed for safeguarding our young people's spiritual moral formation: (1) providing adequate emotional support; (2) demonstrating moral and spiritual excellence in our personal life, choices, values, attitudes, character, and behavior as parents; and (3) situating our family (by way of location, priorities, traditions, boundaries, friendships, etc.) in a way that biblical moral and spiritual values retain an influential edge. Paul's counsel is still apropos: "Fix your thoughts on what is true and honorable and right. Think about things that are pure and lovely and admirable. Think about things that are excellent and worthy of praise" (Phil. 4:8, NLT). "I want you to be wise about what is good, and innocent about what is evil. The God of peace will soon crush Satan under your feet" (Rom. 16:19, 20, NIV). We need to be sensitive to the things that make young people vulnerable in our confusing world with its competing values, priorities, and viewpoints. As parents and adults, we need to be sure that we do not create that vulnerability by our own decisions, attitudes, and actions. On a more practical level, we must ever remember that "things which matter most must never be at the mercy of things which matter least."[31] "Don't let the world around you squeeze you into its own mould," Paul admonishes (Rom. 12:2, Phillips). For some of us that means a reordering of our lives.

While this episode ends without apparent resolution—only alienation, loneliness, fear, and pain, with hurting parents, hurting children, and a hurting community—it does not lack hope. Every parent and every family needs to watch what God does in this heavyhearted moment. Genesis appears to finish this episode with the angry words of Jacob's sons: "Should he treat our sister as a harlot?" (Gen. 34:31, NASB). The very next words, though, continue the story: "Then God said to Jacob, 'Arise, go up to Bethel and live there, and make an altar there to God, who appeared to you when you fled from your brother Esau'" (Gen. 35:1, NASB). Right "then," in that heavyhearted moment of brokenness and fear and alienation, God declares, "It's not too late, Jacob. You can move to a better place. Come worship Me."

The Lord steps into a painful moment of incredible dysfunction and says, "Worship Me. That's the way out, Jacob. Worship. I'm here. Come! Relocate. Get your priorities straight again." Every dysfunctional family, every hurting parent, every broken young person needs to hear these words about our compassionate God. Instead of abandoning us in our family failures and dysfunction, He wants to heal, to forgive, to empower. He desires to save us from that fatal family crash before it's too late.

No matter where you've been, what you've said, what you haven't done, or what your family is like, God promises to come close and to give you resources to begin the healing.

My mother has one of those apocryphal Ellen White statements posted by her telephone. You know, one of those pithy and memorable utterances that someone maintains she wrote, but you nor anyone else has been able to find its source no matter how hard you've searched, even using the computer data base. But it sounds so good, so true, so you cling to it, because it's what you need, even if you know it's likely apocryphal. It goes like this: "The last mediatorial work of Christ before laying aside His priestly garments is to present the prayers of parents for their children, and I saw a Mighty Angel sent out and thousands of children will remember their early training and be brought back just before probation closes." That's the kind of hope every hurting parent longs to have, the kind of promise they yearn to claim. In the end we want our family complete in the kingdom of God. Most of us have to admit that we don't have what it takes. So apocryphal promises like this encourage hope. Although we can't pin the exact wording down anywhere, this statement reflects the incredible yearning of parents and young people alike for God's mercy on behalf of their family.

Without doubt God will do everything possible to assure that our family is complete in His kingdom. He has been working, is working, and will continue to work to the very last to bring our children back. Malachi gives hint of it when he promises: "See, I will send you the prophet Elijah before that great and dreadful day of the Lord comes. He will turn the hearts of the fathers to their children, and the hearts of the children to their fathers" (Mal. 4:5, 6, NIV).

Isaiah is even more specific about God's last-hour intervention for families. Speaking to a generation headed for exile, whose children bore the brunt of their parents' failures and sins, God assures His people Israel that "the children born during your bereavement will yet say in your hearing, 'This place is too small for us; give us more space to live in.' Then you will say in your heart, 'Who bore me these? I was bereaved and barren; I was exiled and rejected. Who brought these up? I was left all alone, but these—where have they come from?' This is what the Sovereign Lord says: 'See, I will beckon to the Gentiles, I will lift up my banner to the peoples; they will bring your sons in their arms and carry your daughters on their shoulders. Kings will be your foster fathers, and their queens your nursing mothers. . . . Then you will know that I am the Lord; those who hope in me will not be disappointed.' Can plunder be taken from warriors, or captives rescued from the fierce? But this is what the Lord says: 'Yes, captives will be taken from warriors, and plunder retrieved from the fierce; I will contend with those who contend with you, and your children I will save'" (Isa. 49:20-25, NIV).

---

[1] See the National Transportation Safety Board final report on the Kennedy crash: www.ntsb.gov/aviation/NYC/99A178.htm; Glen Johnson, "NTSB to Cite Pilot in Kennedy Crash," Associated Press, June 23, 2000; David Ho, "JFK, Jr., Crash Blamed on Pilot Error," Associated Press, July 6, 2000; "Instructors Say Pilot Error Most Likely Cause," Associated Press, July 21, 1999.

[2] See ry[i (`îr) "excitement" and ry[i (`îr) "city": R. Laird Harris, ed., *Theological Wordbook of the Old Testament* (Chicago: Moody Press, 1980), vol. 2, pp. 655, 656, 664, 665.

[3] Scripture records how Lamech takes two wives named Adah ("beauty") and Zillah ("adornment"). The meanings of these names, along with Lamech's polygamy, indicates the values Lamech and his society placed on womanhood and external beauty (Gen. 4:19). But there is also pride and boasting of power and self-assertion as Lamech gloats over being stronger than the young man who wounded him (verses 23, 24).

[4] Jacques Ellul, *The Meaning of the City* (Grand Rapids: William B. Eerdmans Pub. Co., 1970), p. 50. See Ellul's discussion of city in Genesis, pp. 1-20.

[5] E. Roop, *Genesis*, p. 217.

[6] G. Getz, *Jacob*, p. 174.

[7] *Ibid.*, p. 164.

[8] T. Epp, *The God of Jacob*, p. 104.

[9] *Ibid.*, p. 105.

[10] S. Dresner, *Rachel*, p. 64.

[11] *Ibid.*

[12] *Ibid.*

[13] *Ibid.*, p. 65.

[14] Anita Manning, "Absent Dads Scar Millions of Daughters for Life," *USA Today*, June 7, 2000.

[15] H. Norman Wright, *Always Daddy's Girl: Understanding Your Father's Impact on Who You Are* (Ventura, Calif.: Regal Books, 1989), p. 145.

[16] N. Rosenblatt and J. Horwitz, *Wrestling With Angels*, p. 306.

[17] *Roop*, p. 219.

[18] Rosenblatt and Horwitz, p. 307.

[19] *Ibid.*

[20] *Ibid.*

[21] Epp, p. 108.

[22] Roop, p. 221.

[23] Rosenblatt and Horwitz, p. 310.

[24] *Ibid.*

[25] *Ibid.*, p. 312.

[26] Roop, p. 223.

[27] *Ibid.*, p. 221.

[28] Epp, p. 110.

[29] *Ibid.*, p. 111.

[30] Stephen R. Covey, *The 7 Habits of Highly Effective Families* (New York: Franklin Covey, 1997), p. 113.

[31] *Ibid.*, p. 114.

DNA OF CHRISTIAN FAMILY CULTURE

ten

(Genesis 35:1-7)

According to a Federal Aviation Administration advisory circular entitled "'Pilot's Spatial Disorientation,' tests conducted with qualified pilots indicated that it can take as long as 35 seconds to establish full control by instruments after a loss of visual reference of the earth's surface."[1] In other words, once vertigo overtakes a pilot it can take up to 35 seconds to regain correct orientation even with instruments staring them in the face and telling them the truth about their plane's attitude or motion in relation to the earth's surface. When you can't determine if you're climbing or descending, turning or flying level, it's hard to trust your instruments. It's even more difficult to make corrective adjustments in response to those instruments. You have to keep telling yourself that the gauges are right no matter what you think or feel. The instruments are always right! Trust them.

While 35 seconds isn't very long, it's more than the remaining seconds most pilots have before they crash. John F. Kennedy, Jr., obviously didn't have enough time. As we saw earlier, his plane fell 5,000 feet per minute—10 times normal. When you're plummeting that fast, 35 seconds is too long. Only an instantaneous corrective response to instrument readings by an experienced pilot could have made a difference by then. Kennedy should have paid attention to his instruments sooner.

When Jacob pitched his tent outside the city of Shechem, he and his family experienced spiritual vertigo. In the previous chapter we saw how they encountered powerful social forces and cultural values that fundamentally altered their moral and ethical sense of what was, in fact, right. They became disoriented. Shechem threw their moral compass off, and they didn't even know it. As a result, they began a downward moral-spiritual "graveyard spiral" that threatened to destroy not only their family, but their very identity as God's people as well. It was only a matter of time. But God graciously intervened, inviting them to reorient themselves to His moral-spiritual horizon before it was too late. They needed to look at their spiritual-moral instruments and trust them. "Then God said to Jacob, 'Go up to Bethel and settle there, and build an altar there to God, who appeared to you when you were fleeing from your brother Esau'" (Gen. 35:1, NIV).

Stephen Covey tells us that "good families—even great families—are off track 90 percent of the time! The key is that they have a sense of destination. They know what the 'track' looks like. And they keep coming back to it time and time again."[2] It's like the flight of an airplane, he comments. Before takeoff, pilots file a flight plan. They know exactly where they are going. During the flight, however, wind, rain, turbulence, air traffic, human error, and other factors act upon the plane—jostling it slightly in different directions so that most of the time the plane is not even on the prescribed flight path. The entire trip consists of slight deviations from the flight plan. Sometimes weather systems or unusually heavy air traffic may even cause major reroutings. During them all pilots make constant adjustments so that time and time again they return to their flight plan. "The hope lies not in the deviations but in the vision, the plan, and the ability to get back on track."[3] Jacob's family not only needed to look at their instruments in order to avert total disaster at Shechem; they needed a flight plan that would guide them to a better place, a better experience.

BEAUTIFUL FAMILY CULTURE

As it says in Proverbs: "Where there is no vision, the people perish" (Prov. 29:18). I suggest that where there is no vision or purpose—

flight plan—the Christian family perishes. As Covey writes, we need to "begin with the end in mind."[4] Having your destination clearly in mind affects every decision along the way. The opposite is also true. If we have no mental creation, no envisioning of the future—just let life happen, let ourselves be swept along with the flow of society's values and trends without having any sense of vision or purpose—we will only perish. We need to be asking ourselves: "What is the purpose of our family? What is our (this) family about? Where are we heading? When we get where we are going, where will we be and will we really want to be there?"

Often we read Psalm 127 in the context of family: "Without the help of the Lord, it is useless to build a home or to guard a city. It is useless to get up early and stay up late in order to earn a living. God takes care of His own even while they sleep. Children are a gift from the Lord; they are a real blessing. The sons of a man when he is young are like arrows in a soldier's hand. Happy is the man who has many such arrows in his quiver. He will never be defeated when he contends with his enemies at the gate" (verses 1-5, paraphrase). This psalm not only reminds us that our families need God's help and blessing in order to be successful in the world; it points to a fundamental solidarity of family against its enemies as well. You'll notice that the word "picture" here is that of a warrior with arrows in his hand. Arrows are weapons. An archer uses them in battle, directing them toward a target—the enemy. Not only are parents responsible for the direction of their children; such children are "living assets"[5] (both offensive and defensive) in the battle against that family's moral-spiritual (and physical) enemies. Scripture and society view children as part of the family arsenal against its foes.

My wife and I have some evangelical Christian friends who see their family in a direct offensive struggle against a fallen world. Through their family they are staking out a claim for God's kingdom in the world. They take Psalm 127 serious. In their opinion, one way you fight an evil culture is through a solid, evangelical Christian home—specifically raising godly children who stand out in bold relief against the evil around them. The family now has 10 such offspring arrows in their quiver. The parents regard each child as a part of their work for Christ in a confused and dying world. Talk about purpose, vision, and reason for being! The challenge is not only for parents to have such a vision themselves, but to raise their children to share that vision with them.

Covey writes of the need for families to develop a "beautiful family culture."[6] When he uses the word "culture," he is talking about the "spirit of the family," the character of the family in terms of its depth, quality, and maturity of relationships. According to Covey, a beautiful family culture is a "we" culture.[7] Whatever a family's culture is, stands for, and does in terms of its values and priorities and traditions, it is a shared vision, purpose, and experience. It is not just that of mom and dad or empty tradition, but belongs to everyone, is experienced by everyone, and is valued by everyone. Each family member has had a part in some way in its formation. What makes family culture beautiful, according to Covey, is the "we."

While Covey's vision of "we" family culture includes Christian values, such a beautiful family culture could be expressed in a Muslim or Buddhist or nonreligious home. For Covey the guiding principle is "we," rather than what that "we" envisions. While I affirm Covey's notion of a "we" family culture, I believe our families need to develop this sense of "we" in the context of a Christian family culture. Not only am I thinking of the moral and spiritual orientation of the family as decidedly Christian; I will go further and call for a decidedly Adventist Christian perspective. But how does it happen? Jacob's summons to worship God at Bethel provides some insights. Up until now, he had not filed a family flight plan, but things were about to change.

TAKING THE LEAD

First, parents themselves must hear God's call to create a family flight plan and understand the importance to do so. Parents must take the lead. "Then God said to Jacob, 'Go up to Bethel and settle there, and build an altar there to God, who appeared to you when you were fleeing from your brother Esau.' So Jacob said to his household and to all who were with him, 'Get rid of the foreign gods you have with you, and purify yourselves and change your clothes. Then come, let us go up to Bethel, where I will build an altar to God, who answered me in the day of my distress and who has been with me wherever I have gone.' So they gave Jacob all the foreign gods they had and the rings in their ears, and Jacob buried them under the oak at Shechem. Then they set out, and the terror of God fell upon the towns all around them so that no one pursued them. Jacob and all the people with him came to Luz (that is, Bethel) in the land of Canaan. There he built an altar, and he called the place El Bethel, because it was there that God revealed himself to him when he was fleeing from his brother" (Gen. 35:1-7, NIV).

One gets the impression that Jacob had never taken real spiritual leadership in his home. Until now he had not filed a family flight plan. In many respects, everyone in the family was doing what was right in their own eyes. Perhaps Jacob was so busy dealing with his own inner struggles that he either forgot or overlooked or didn't have the resources for developing a godly family culture. It is clear that he had not led everyone in his family to forsake the gods of Mesopotamia. In fact, his favorite wife, Rachel, seemed enamored with pagan idols, something that he had apparently allowed to continue. In fact, "she may have been a negative witness to the rest of Jacob's household"[8] and likely stymied his attempts to draw them to God. "Most of Jacob's family probably still dabbled in their pagan religions."[9] Jacob had yet to help his family commit totally to the living God of heaven.

Now God once more, and with great emphasis, invited Jacob to return to Bethel—to worship. While the invitation came to Jacob personally, he interpreted it in the context of family: "So Jacob said to his household and to all who were with him, 'Get rid of the foreign gods you have with you, and purify yourselves and change your clothes. Then come, let us go up to Bethel.'" "Let us go," Jacob said. Following the events at Shechem, he understood, as he had never done before, that his family needed radical reorientation. He was willing now, to take the lead. But to make a difference, it had to be something they did together. Purposeful and godly family culture will never develop until parents hear the call to develop a family flight plan. They must set the pace and assume the initiative. It's not enough for them to do it on behalf of the family.

TELLING OUR STORY

Second, Jacob shared his own experience through personal testimony: "Let us arise and go up to Bethel, and I will make an altar there to God, who answered me in the day of my distress and has been with me wherever I have gone" (verse 3, NASB).

"We're going to Bethel!" Jacob declared.

"Where?" they undoubtedly asked.

"Bethel."

"Bethel? Why Bethel?"

"I'm going back to where I first found God."

"What do you mean? When did you find God?"

"Jacob was telling them something they had probably never heard before."[10] Twenty years before, he had met God on a cold dark night when in the loneliness of his failures his tormented heart had cried out for help, mercy, and blessing. God graciously answered his distress with a vision of mighty angels ascending and descending on a ladder linking heaven and earth. Jacob's family may have heard bits and pieces of the story before, but certainly not as on this occasion. The patriarch now opened his inner private world in personal testimony, and it had a profound impact.

In *Patriarchs and Prophets* Ellen White illumines the biblical record: "*With deep emotion* Jacob repeated the story of his first visit to Bethel, when he left his father's tent a lonely wanderer, fleeing for his life, and how the Lord had appeared to him in the night vision. *As he reviewed the wonderful dealings of God with him, his own heart was softened, his children also were touched by a subduing power;* he had taken the most effectual way to prepare them to join in the worship of God when they should arrive in Bethel. 'And they gave unto Jacob all the strange gods which were in their hand, and all their earrings which were in their ears; and Jacob hid them under the oak which was by Shechem.'"[11]

Jacob shared his spiritual journey with deep emotion. In the process it affected his own heart and drew his children into the testimony as a "subduing power" touched them.

We can think of several reasons Jacob's family was in a mood to listen and respond to this call to worship—to reorient their lives and file a new flight plan. "Everyone . . . was well aware of what had just happened in Shechem."[12] Jacob raised the possibility of retaliation on the part of neighboring clans. No doubt, some may have even been assembling forces in order to attack. "Pragmatically, they all knew time was of the essence. They could be attacked at any moment. But Jacob's sincere witness regarding the God of Bethel must have touched their hearts."[13] It was a deciding factor.

Irrespective of why Jacob's family was in a listening mood, this moment of personal testimony proved to be an occasion of family spiritual renewal, a time of purposeful consecration and worship. The same subduing power touched each family member present. As each one witnessed Jacob's moving testimony, they began removing certain garments and idols and pieces of jewelry from their lives in an act of consecration and worship.

Why did Jacob's family obey him and share in the renewing experience? Why were they now obedient rather than rebellious? Because he was being direct about spiritual things, sharing from his own heart and giving directions as to what every one of them should do in relation to God's call to worship. At last he was assuming spiritual leadership. You can't get more straightforward and unequivocal when you say, "Get rid of the foreign gods you have with you, and purify yourselves and change your clothes." Furthermore, nothing is more gripping than personal testimony shared from a softened, Spirit-filled heart. One of the biggest struggles Christian parents have is conveying their spiritual passion to the next generation. Nothing unlocks that passion more in the imagination of young people than when parents tell their story—really share it—and in the process reveal not only their inner private world but give heartfelt witness to the living God who has answered them in their personal distress. No beautiful family culture is possible without open parental hearts. The privacy we are so inclined to cling to stifles spiritual passion in our homes. We need a new boldness to pray openly, to be out in the open spiritually, to unreservedly share ourselves and our journey of faith, and to reveal how passionately important God really is in our lives.

CHOOSING THE BEST

In his heart Jacob knew that he and his family could not approach God in worship while pagan influences, moral compromises, and spiritual indifference filled their lives. As we have suggested, "apparently a number of people in Jacob's household had an array of gods, including other sacred ornaments. Among these ornaments were earrings that were worn by both men and women." [14] Most likely people considered them magical and used them for divine protection. They represented a false view of God as well as a false experience with Him. Now in this solemn moment of family spiritual revival and consecration we hear Jacob saying: " 'Put away the foreign gods which are among you, and purify yourselves and change your garments; and let us arise and go up to Bethel, and I will make an altar there to God, who answered me in the day of my distress, and has been with me wherever I have gone.' So they gave to Jacob all the foreign gods which they had, and the rings which were in their ears; and Jacob hid them under the oak which was near Shechem" (Gen. 35:2-4, NASB).

Think for a moment about what was happening. As each one witnessed firsthand their father's moving testimony, they began removing certain garments and idols and pieces of jewelry from their lives in an act of consecration and worship. They were radically adjusting their lives as well as their theology. [15] In the process they displayed two moral spiritual truths. First, the artistic and tangible expressions of culture that people wear and adorn themselves with are *value-laden*. They express moral or spiritual concepts that the wearer wittingly or unwittingly identifies with. Their sense of self, value system, and view of God is somehow locked up in these concrete expressions.

Second, genuine consecration to God expresses itself through shedding those cultural idioms that might convey ungodly values. Consecration to God includes external forms. While you can have the external forms in your life without consecration, you cannot have consecration without it affecting those external forms that in one way or another either nurture or compete with that very consecration. Doing and being are inseparably linked, a moral and spiritual truth portrayed at Shechem. Shechem represented a world civilization filled with tangible cultural expressions laden with pagan values and ideals.[16] A new God-focused family culture—their new flight plan—demanded a distinct break with the pagan values and ideals of Shechem. That meant shedding those cultural expressions that conveyed ungodly values and competed with their commitment to God.

Jacob asked his family to put away their foreign gods, cleanse themselves, and change their garments. And they did. Then they journeyed to Bethel and worshiped. Undoubtedly it may have been the very first time Jacob's family experienced the "we" of beautiful family culture that Covey speaks about. Together they chose a God-informed family culture over the culture of their world. Rejecting tangible cultural expressions loaded with pagan values and ideals, they conformed their personal and family life to the kind of consecration consistent with worshiping God.

Parents often walk on eggshells when it comes to calling for specific behavior. Not wanting to be offensive or legalistic but desiring their family to operate by principles rather than rules, they attempt to give their children room to think and choose for themselves and not drive them away. Covey, however, asserts that "with a clear sense of shared vision and values, you can be very demanding when it comes to standards."[17] Likewise, there can be a powerful bonding between parents and children and husbands and wives that simply does not exist without shared moral-spiritual vision and values. The bottom line comes down to the reality that "you cannot . . . stay where you are, and go with God."[18] Choosing the best family culture means adjusting your life to God. You conform your viewpoints to His and modify your ways to be like His ways. The adjusting is always to a

Person, but it is tangible and concrete. It has to do with values. While God comes to us where we are and receives us where we are, He never leaves us there. You cannot follow God and remain in the same place. For the first time Jacob was willing to call for a more concrete expression of commitment, surrender, and obedience. Because his personal testimony had stirred their spiritual imagination, his family for the first time was ready to bring their lifestyle and religious experience into harmony with their relationship with the living God of heaven. They chose the best.

NAMING A FAMILY

"Once Jacob's family had packed all their belongings, loaded their camels, and corralled all their livestock, they headed off for Bethel. . . . God honored their obedience with supernatural protection."[19] "Then they set out, and the terror of God fell upon the towns all around them so that no one pursued them" (Gen. 35:5, NIV). The Lord was "demonstrating that they needed only Him for . . . guidance and protection—not the false gods and other assorted religious paraphernalia that they had brought with them from Paddan-Aram."[20] Finally they arrived at Bethel where Jacob built an altar and named the place El Bethel (the God of Bethel), because God had appeared to him there at Bethel when he was fleeing from Esau. Here at Bethel "God appeared to him again and blessed him. God said to him, 'Your name is Jacob, but you will no longer be called Jacob; your name will be Israel.' So he named him Israel. And God said to him, 'I am God Almighty; be fruitful and increase in number. A nation and a community of nations will come from you, and kings will come from your body. The land I gave to Abraham and Isaac I also give to you, and I will give this land to your descendants after you.' Then God went up from him at the place where he had talked with him. Jacob set up a stone pillar at the place where God had talked with him, and he poured out a drink offering on it; he also poured oil on it. Jacob called the place where God had talked with him Bethel" (verses 9-15, NIV).

Jacob's return to Bethel brought a new and deeper experience with God. It was also a moment when the Lord formally changed his name to Israel. But even though the text says "God appeared to [Jacob]," the context includes the whole family. It is the only place where we find a whole family coming with a patriarch to an occasion of God's appearance. In a sense God names a family, not only an individual, Israel. It is a people (a family), not a single person, who will carry God's promises into the future.[21]

Israel becomes the common name given to Jacob's descendants. Scripture calls the whole people of the 12 tribes "Israel," "Israelites," the "children of Israel," and the "house of Israel" (Gen. 47:27; 49:7; 50:25; Ex. 1:7, 9; Joshua 3:17; 7:25; Judges 8:27; Jer. 3:21; Ex. 16:31; 40:38). When referring to Jacob's descendants, the Bible often uses Israel interchangeably with the name Jacob: "But now, listen to me, Jacob my servant, Israel my chosen one. The Lord who made you and helps you says: O Jacob, my servant, do not be afraid. O Israel, my chosen one, do not fear. For I will give you abundant water to quench your thirst and to moisten your parched fields. And I will pour out my Spirit and my blessings on your children. They will thrive like watered grass, like willows on a riverbank. Some will proudly claim, 'I belong to the Lord.' Others will say, 'I am a descendant of Jacob.' Some will write the Lord's name on their hands and will take the honored name of Israel as their own" (Isa. 44:1-5, NLT).

Specifically, Israel as a covenant name signifies an experience with God and includes family identity, purpose, mission, and culture. "'You shall be to Me a kingdom of priests and a holy nation.' These are the words that you shall speak to the sons of Israel," God tells Moses (Ex. 19:6, NASB). The prophet Isaiah states: "It is too small a thing for you to be my servant to restore the tribes of Jacob and bring back those of Israel I have kept. I will also make you a light for the Gentiles, that you may bring my salvation to the ends of the earth" (Isa. 49:6, NIV; see Isa. 42:6; 60:1-3). God's naming of Jacob (and thus his family) as Israel points to his/their purpose of blessing and saving mankind.[22] To have a saving influence in the world by touching all people with God's grace was Jacob's family mission statement, their reason for existence.

Begin with the end in mind, Covey writes. Create a clear, compelling vision of what you and your family are all about. Having your destination clearly in mind affects every decision along the way. Each of us should put biblical principles and a relationship with God ahead of each other and ahead of our family. By creating a social will to be faithful to God in our lives and in our relationships with one another, we will be living witnesses of His grace and a blessing to those outside our families. Such a family purpose or mission "literally becomes the DNA of family life."[23] As the chromosomal structure inside each cell of the body represents the blueprint of the entire body—and not only defines the function of that cell but also how it relates to every other cell—having a shared vision will create deep bonding. A shared vision and identity provides a sense of unity and purpose that is so powerful, so cohesive, so motivating that it literally pulls people together with a purpose strong enough to transcend the challenges of daily living, the baggage of the past, and the all-pervading influence of Shechem's culture. This is what God wants for your family. You need to create a family mission statement if your family is going to survive Shechem and keep on track to the kingdom.

I've witnessed the power of such conscious family vision. For example, I experienced it during the wedding of some friends. Of all the weddings I have ever attended, this ceremony was truly an act of worship. Both parents of the bride and the groom, as well as grandparents, shared a series of litanies and messages that focused on marriage as a covenant relationship with the purpose of glorifying God and serving others. "Almighty Father: We praise You for uniting families through the marriage of Ruth and Boaz and for bringing the Messiah through that union. We thank You for bringing two families together today. We pray that You will bless and use the union of Kristin and Adam for the upbuilding of Your church on earth and the hastening of Your heavenly kingdom. Amen," the congregation read at one point. "Go forth in the strength of the Lord to love and serve each other, your fellow human beings, and your God," their mothers charged at the close.

Another time I witnessed thoughtful family vision during a

Sabbath morning child dedication. One of the young couples in our church named their firstborn son Rayne. When you hear that little guy's name you immediately think "rain" and instinctively ask, "How do you spell that?" It's purposeful. This couple wants you to think "rain" when you hear their son's name. And they want him to think "rain" as part of his identity. The child's parents look forward to the outpouring of the latter rain in the last days. They envision the promised time of Holy Spirit empowering that brings the final harvest of our world through the loud cry of the angel of Revelation 18 that lightens the whole world. They not only want to experience the latter rain power of the Holy Spirit for themselves; they are praying that their son and his generation will be at the forefront of such passionate proclaiming of the third angel's message. The entire moment of dedication revolved around this hope and vision for this boy's spiritual life, power, and witness.

This kind of family vision touches every aspect of a family's (or couple's) psyche, including values, money, friends, pleasure, possessions, work, and worship. Beginning with the end in mind enables you to identify the principles that will help you get there. "In reality, the ends and the means—the destination and the journey—are the same."[24] The ends and the means are inseparable. Our quest for eternity with our family demands choices consistent with that vision. God is there both to inspire and to empower such vision.

IT CAN HAPPEN EVEN AT SHECHEM

"The place Shechem figures prominently in the history . . . of Israel."[25] The site was the first place where Abraham had set up an altar when he journeyed into Canaan (Gen. 12:6, 7). Here Jacob too built an altar, but also put his family at extreme spiritual risk by settling his family there. Shechem is the place where the children of Israel buried Joseph when they finally settled in Canaan following the Exodus (Joshua 24:32). Eventually Shechem became one of the cities of refuge, the central city of refuge for western Palestine (Joshua 20:7). It was the site of the well Jacob dug, and where the Samaritan woman heard Jesus point to Himself as the water of life (John 4:5).

Joshua called all the children of Israel to Shechem for a time of decision and commitment: "'So honor the Lord and serve him wholeheartedly. Put away forever the idols your ancestors worshiped when they lived beyond the Euphrates River and in Egypt. Serve the Lord alone. But if you are unwilling to serve the Lord, then choose today whom you will serve. Would you prefer the gods your ancestors served beyond the Euphrates? Or will it be the gods of the Amorites in whose land you now live? But as for me and my family, we will serve the Lord.' The people replied, 'We would never forsake the Lord and worship other gods. . . . We, too, will serve the Lord, for he alone is our God. . . . We are determined to serve the Lord!' 'You are accountable for this decision,' Joshua said. 'You have chosen to serve the Lord.' 'Yes,' they replied, 'we are accountable.' 'All right then,' Joshua said, 'destroy the idols among you, and turn your hearts to the Lord, the God of Israel.' The people said to Joshua, 'We will serve the Lord our God. We will obey him alone.' So Joshua made a covenant with the people that day at Shechem, committing them to a permanent and binding contract between themselves and the Lord" (Joshua 24:14-25, NLT).

This place where Jacob's family nearly failed is linked with rich spiritual imagery and decision. At Shechem Jacob's family plunged headlong into the world, nearly losing their identity as God's people. But there he and his family made their decision to listen to their instruments and file a flight plan before it was too late. They removed everything from their lives that was inconsistent with their call to worship and honor God. Jacob hid these tangible expressions of decision in the ground under the landmark oak tree near the city. As they buried their past they took on a new identity, new purpose, and new resolve. No longer in a nose dive, they were at last following God's plan. Such was Joshua's call to a later generation of Israel. The issues have always been the same—the flight plan, the purpose, identity, and culture of the people of God. God's people will always have a tangible forsaking and laying aside of things as they tune their hearts more fully to God and His purposes.

We can make decisions for God even at Shechem. The place of

near failure can be the site of new resolve no matter how off track your family has gone. Even if, like Jacob, you never really had a flight plan, no statement of purpose, no clear Christian or Adventist identity, it is never too late to reorient yourself with a sense of shared purpose.

Through the story of Jacob and his family God is preaching a gospel of recovery. "The God of Jacob is preeminently the God of the second chance to the Christian who has failed persistently. The second—or twenty-second—chance does not necessarily avert the temporal consequences of past failure, but even failure can be a stepping stone to new victories. God wastes nothing, not even failure."[26] That is true for our families as well.

What is the purpose of your family? What is it all about? Where are you heading together? When you get where you are going, where will your family be? Will it be where you really want your family to be? "Where there is no vision the people perish" (Prov. 29:18). Where there is no vision the Adventist Christian family perishes. Begin your family's journey with the end in mind. And be sure to put the first things first. Let the grip of Jacob's God summon you to a new experience of spiritual life, purposeful consecration, and worship.

---

[1] See the National Transportation Safety Board final report on the Kennedy crash: www.ntsb.gov/aviation/NYC/99A178.htm; G. Johnson, "NTSB to Cite Pilot in Kennedy Crash," Associated Press, June 23, 2000; D. Ho, "JFK Jr. Crash Blamed on Pilot Error," Associated Press, July 6, 2000; "Instructors Say Pilot Error Most Likely Cause," Associated Press, July 21, 1999.

[2] S. Covey, *The 7 Habits of Highly Effective Families*, p. 9.

[3] *Ibid.*, p. 10.

[4] *Ibid.*, p. 71.

[5] Derek Kidner, *Psalms 73-150: A Commentary on Books III-V of the Psalms* (Downers Grove, Ill.: InterVarsity Press, 1975), p. 441.

[6] Covey, p. 20.

[7] *Ibid.*

[8] G. Getz, *Jacob*, p. 169.

[9] *Ibid.*

[10] *Ibid.*

[11] E. G. White, *Patriarchs and Prophets*, pp. 205, 206. (Italics supplied.)

[12] Getz, p. 170.

[13] *Ibid.*

[14] *Ibid.*

[15] "They actually turned these 'protective' ornaments over to Jacob in the midst of impending doom and in the process they literally traded a false view of God for a right understanding" (Getz, p. 171).

[16] For an extended discussion on these two principles, see my chapter on cultural assim-

ilation, "If You Know Everything There Is to Know About Timbuktu" in Larry L. Lichtenwalter, *Out of the Pit* (Hagerstown, Md.: Review and Herald Pub. Assn., 2000), pp. 80-93.

[17] Covey, p. 95.

[18] Henry T. Blackaby and Claude V. King, *Experiencing God: Knowing and Doing the Will of God* (Nashville: LifeWay Press, 1990), p. 127.

[19] Getz, p. 171.

[20] *Ibid.*

[21] E. Roop, *Genesis,* p. 226.

[22] Hans K. LaRondelle, *The Israel of God in Prophecy* (Berrien Springs, Mich.: Andrews University Press, 1983), pp. 91-96.

[23] Covey, p. 97.

[24] *Ibid.,* p. 78.

[25] Roop, p. 217.

[26] J. O. Sanders, *Spiritual Manpower,* p. 36.

eleven

OH, RACHEL! MOMENTS OF LOSS, SEASONS OF GRIEF

(Genesis 35:9-20)

O ne hundred sixty-eight bronze-and-glass chairs honor the 168 people killed in the bombing of the Alfred P. Murrah Federal Building in Oklahoma City on April 19, 1995. The chairs are positioned on a grass lawn in rows that correspond to the floors of the building where the victims were when the bomb exploded. The second row—representing the day-care center on the second floor—has smaller chairs. "Five chairs located off to the side, west of the others, are for those who died outside the building. They are positioned on a slight rise leading to a scarred wall—all that is left of the building—and look down to a long black reflecting pool, three quarters of an inch deep and flush against the surrounding granite pathway of stones salvaged from the rubble.

"On the far side of the pool stand fledgling trees, the 'Rescuers' Orchard,' and a magnificent 'Survivor Tree,' for those who lived through the blast and for the act of survival itself. Scorched and stripped of leaves by the bombing, it now shimmers with a rich green. The memorial is framed by two massive bronze entrance gates: the 9:01 Gate and the 9:03 Gate, the lettering done like a digital clock. The minutes signify the times just before and after the explosion."[1] The chairs represent the moment of 9:02.

Lights in the bases of the chairs burn 24 hours a day, and as dusk falls upon the memorial each chair has a haunting glow. "To see those chairs lighted," commented Oklahoma governor Frank Keating, "makes you understand that each chair is a symbol of a human life lost. The hillside of lights is overwhelming. I met a woman who lost her father in the bombing, and I expressed my sympathy. But she seemed to take solace from the chairs, and unlike some others, she did sit in the chair with her father's name on it. She told me, 'It's like sitting in my dad's lap. Like being a little girl again.'"[2]

Jeanine Gist, who had a part in the memorial design, finds it hard to look at the chairs. A blow to the back of the head by a flying object killed her daughter Karen. The woman's body was found intact, seated on her chair in her office. "You see them [the chairs], and you understand the impact of loss," she says.[3] At holidays and special family moments she keeps an empty chair at the table.

When Rachel died en route to Ephrath (modern Bethlehem), "Jacob raised a monument on her grave" (Gen. 35:20, New Jerusalem). It was something to remember the tragic moment of her death, something that would etch Rachel forever in human memory. He succeeded. Genesis attests the persistence of Rachel's monument by the unusual phrase "that same monument of Rachel's Tomb which is there today" (verse 20, New Jerusalem). It alerts us to the timeless quality of her grave.[4] In fact, it is one of the few burial sites whose prominence has remained throughout history. Three thousand years ago the book of Samuel recorded it as a well-known landmark (1 Sam. 10:2). Today *Kever* Rachel, as her grave is called, is a prominent and emotionally charged shrine in Israeli psyche. Thousands of pilgrims from near and far come yearly to visit, pray, reflect, hope.[5]

Jacob was on his way home after 20 years. By now he had broken free from Laban's grasping hand and was wealthy beyond compare (Gen. 30:43). Reconciled with Esau and receiving a new name from God Himself—Israel (Gen. 35:10)—he had succeeded in getting his family identity and purpose back on track. With the arrival of Rachel's son, Joseph, Leah no longer posed a threat to household peace. The promise of land and God's blessings were ringing in Jacob's ears: "I am God Almighty. Multiply and fill the earth! Become a great nation, even many nations. Kings will be among your descendants! And I will pass on to you the land I gave to Abraham and Isaac.

Yes, I will give it to you and your descendants" (verses 11, 12, NLT).

Jacob looked forward to a joyous meeting with his aging father Isaac. It is at this very moment of promise that Jacob experienced "the darkest tragedy of his life, a tragedy from which he never recovers."[6]

They had set out from Bethel toward what is now modern-day Bethlehem. Somewhere along the way Rachel went into heavy labor with her second child. When her labor was at its hardest, the midwife tried to encourage her, saying, " 'Do not worry, this is going to be another boy.' At the moment when she breathed her last, for she was dying, she named him Ben-Oni [son of my sorrow]. His father, however, named him Benjamin [son of my right hand]. So Rachel died and was buried on the road to Ephrath, now Bethlehem. Jacob raised a monument on her grave, that same monument of Rachel's Tomb which is there today" (verses 17-20, New Jerusalem).

Scripture tells us that Rachel's death was painful and protracted. According to medical authorities, a careful study of the text suggests that the birth was likely in an impacted breech position in which the rear end of the infant appears first, with the legs drawn up against the stomach. "This possibly would explain how the midwife knew the baby's gender during the birth and why the process was so prolonged and so painful. . . . It would also suggest a plausible cause of death—fatal hemorrhage resulting presumably from the midwife's tearing of the uterus."[7]

REFUSING TO BE COMFORTED

The sudden death of a loved one—a spouse, a child, a parent— is a crushing blow. In addition to shock, deep grief, and numbness, one has to deal with the aftermath emotions of depression, guilt, and loneliness. The loss of a loved one without warning always leaves the haunting feeling of unfinished personal business—plans that will never be realized, endearments left unspoken, emotional conflicts that may never be resolved. Jacob experienced it all.

The patriarch had to deal with the soul-shattering experience of having his beloved Rachel die an agonizing and protracted death filled with pain and fear and hurried exchanges. On top of that he had to come to grips with Rachel's emotionally charged words of how sorrowful her life had been. With life literally draining from her body, Rachel named her newborn son Ben-Oni, "son of my sorrow." Her husband recognized that the name reached beyond the moment of hard labor and untimely death. It expressed a life of disappointment, pain, loneliness, and sorrow. She was telling him how she felt. Rachel obviously believed that she had never had the intimacy, contentment, sense of worth, or blessing she sought—and what Jacob had intended. The woman had forever been caught up in rivalry with Leah and the reality of her own barrenness. And as her life was slipping away Rachel realized without a doubt that she would never have what she yearned for most. Her dreams would never be fulfilled. Leah would win after all.

Jacob didn't like the name "son of my sorrow" and changed it to Benjamin, "son of my right hand," instead. But the reality that Rachel died unfulfilled, unhappy, and sad haunted him the rest of his life. Had he failed her through all those years? Talk about wrestling!

Her lonely burial outside Bethlehem magnified the pathos of Rachel's death.[8] "She would remain alone forever in her roadside grave."[9] Accounts from the wagon trains that crossed America's heartland to the frontiers of Oregon and California contain countless painful moments of loss and roadside burial. Many a parent or spouse would drive away haunted with the image of wild animals digging up the shallow graves. Closure to their grief would be difficult because of the obscurity or unloveliness or loneliness of the place.

When my father-in-law, David Baasch, died unexpectedly with a heart attack, we confronted such a reality. The heavens unleashed a torrent of rain the day we buried Dad—mirroring our anguished hearts. Unexpectedly Dad received a site right on the fence of a busy metropolitan street. Beer cans and litter lay everywhere just beyond the chain-linked barrier. Cars rushed by. Horns blew. And the drenching rain. It was so unlike Dad, who loved nature and order, beauty and stillness. We returned to our home numb, where we sat for hours, asking how we could ever live with this incongruity, this indignity, this irreverent roadside. Dad deserved better! And so months later, on a sunny afternoon, we quietly buried Dad again on a beautiful Vermont hill overlooking the kind of serenity we yearned for him to have as he rests from his labors now and he will experience alive forever when Jesus comes again. Our family needed that kind of closure. But it was a closure Jacob would never have.

Rachel's death was one of his deepest sorrows and his greatest loss. His grief radically changed his life forever. It literally immobilized him. So stark was his agony that he was simply unable to act. Dresner puts it in perspective for us: "The death of Rachel is the watershed in the life of Jacob. From this point on, Jacob, the bright, ambitious son of Isaac, who matched wits with crafty Laban, won Rachel, beheld the mighty ladder, overcame the angel, received the promise of the Lord and the blessing of Abraham, the brilliant prince who victoriously returns home to enter into his inheritance—this same Jacob, after the death of his darling Rachel, withdraws into virtual oblivion. We read no more of power and wealth or encounters with angels, no more of heroic tales to add to the record of his life. Only sorrow, sorrow so unremitting that it carries him all the way to the grave. Overnight he falls into depression. . . . Although capable of fathering children, Jacob has no more with Leah, nor does he take another wife after Rachel's death."[10] The next decades are a tale of pathos and sorrow.

The single most important ingredient in the grieving process is an emotional support network—or at least, one person who can lend a patient and sympathetic ear. But Jacob found himself "totally alone to grieve the loss of his beloved wife. Leah certainly wouldn't want to listen to Jacob mourn her departed rival. Leah's sons, who resented Rachel and the special place she held in their father's heart, would offer little comfort."[11] Rachel's son Joseph was barely a teenager, Benjamin a motherless newborn. So the patriarch remained alone in his grief. Maybe that's why he would say decades later, "Rachel died, to my sorrow" (Gen. 48:7, NASB). "His words *Meytah alai—To me, she died,* . . . imply 'Only I knew the fullness of this sorrow.'"[12] That's how Jacob felt—abandoned in his grief. No one else could ever understand. Christian counselor Norman Wright tells us that people tend to grieve by themselves. It's one of the myths about loss—grieve by yourself.

Not only did Jacob grieve alone, but he refused to be comforted. When years later he held Joseph's blood-soaked tunic after the young man's disappearance, "Jacob tore his clothes and put sackcloth on his loins, and mourned for his son many days. Then all his sons and all his daughters arose to comfort him, but he refused to be comforted. And he said, 'Surely I will go down to Sheol in mourning for my son'" (Gen. 37:34, 35, NASB). Never accepting Joseph's death, he would not allow himself to be consoled. He steeled his heart against any solace and held on to his hurt no matter what. It was a well-developed pattern that began with Rachel's death. His way of handling loss was to reject comforting. Sometimes we feel that dealing with the loss is more painful than the loss itself, so we seal it off as protection. A long-time friend of mine was dying of terminal cancer. One evening as we talked on the phone she shared how her husband was already distancing himself from her, leaving her even more alone in her painful journey toward death. "I guess it'll be easier to grieve if he isn't too close anymore," she sighed. As I said, sometimes we feel that dealing with the loss is more painful than the actual loss, so we wall it off.

In an e-mail just two months after the loss of her husband, my wife's sister vividly shared the pain of loss. "On the morning of July 13 John's death ripped half of the flesh of my body away, leaving a huge, raw, open, bleeding wound, from the top of my head to the bottom of my left pinkie toe. Over the days that followed, the bleeding slowed (no, I didn't bleed to death, though that would have been a peaceful option), and scabs started to form. And I've been walking around with these gross, stinky scabs ever since. But the skin under them has started to heal and itch, and little itty bit by little bit I am peeling those scabs off from the edges. Underneath I am seeking new pink skin. At this rate it'll be years before all the scabs are gone, but I already can see one thing: the skin is *so* scarred, and it will always be that way as long as I live."

GOOD GRIEF?

Jacob's loss soon had profound consequences for his entire family. His unconsoled grief generated some unhealthy patterns of behavior that embroiled his family in even worse dysfunction. Like many bereaved spouses, Jacob transferred his emotional attachment to the most tangible link to his dead wife—her child Joseph.[13] Perhaps the boy resembled Rachel so much—Scripture uses the same adjectives to describe each of them (Gen. 29:17; 39:6)—that whenever Jacob beheld the handsome face of his son, it momentarily comforted him for her loss. In the process, though, he exhibited both favoritism and insensitivity.

Jacob "loved Joseph more than all his sons, because he was the son of his old age; and he made him a varicolored tunic. His brothers saw that their father loved him more than all his brothers; and so they hated him and could not speak to him on friendly terms" (Gen. 37:3, 4, NASB). Clearly he treated Joseph, one of the youngest of his sons, as the eldest, because he was the firstborn of Rachel, whom alone Jacob called "my wife" (Gen. 44:27). It must have been clear, even in Joseph's early years, that Jacob considered the son of his beloved Rachel as deserving of the birthright. That fact caused bitter resentments, jealousy, anger, and hatred that escalated out of control to the point at which it led the brothers to sell Joseph into slavery. When his sons told Jacob that Joseph was dead, he again refused to be comforted. "Jacob's mourning for Joseph is part of his mourning for Rachel—Rachel has died, and now Rachel's child has died."[14]

That's how Judah understood it years later when he pleaded with Egypt's prime minister (not knowing it was Joseph) to spare Benjamin: "Then my father said to us, 'You know that my wife had two sons, and that one of them went away and never returned—doubtless torn to pieces by some wild animal. I have never seen him since. If you take away his brother from me, too, and any harm comes to him, you would bring my gray head down to the grave in deep sorrow.' And now, my lord, I cannot go back without the boy. Our father's life is bound up in the boy's life. When he sees that the boy is not with us, our father will die" (verses 27-31, NLT). Jacob's grief-evoked favoritism accompanied a tacit insensitivity to Leah's sons—to everyone in the family, for that matter. It was as if no one else mattered.

The principle is true—hurting people hurt people. Grieving

people unwittingly and sometimes purposely injure others simply because they hurt. Sometimes it comes because we are afraid to get close. Loss and grief can shut us down and lead us toward unhealthy choices that play out in the interpersonal relationships of our families. "Unresolved grief multiplies problems."[15] It can generate a host of dysfunctional behavior. Jacob expressed most of the classical unhealthy manifestations of grief: suppression of emotions; refusal to be comforted; extended indecisiveness; altered relationships; favoritism; permissiveness; insensitivity toward others who are hurting; anger; and impatience.[16]

Jacob did not have good grief! For the most part it was unhealthy. As we read his story Scripture helps us by showing us what *not* to do. Most people do not know how to grieve. Jacob didn't. When we see how the grief evoked dysfunction in his life and family, it motivates us to find a better way. We must find the mirror opposites and live according to them. But sometimes to do so, we need the help of others.

Loss is an unavoidable and always painful part of life. It usually brings with it the intense emotional suffering we call grief. Such loss can be concrete as with a death in the family, a friend's moving away, our home's burning down, demotion, divorce, or terminal illness. And it can also be abstract (the loss of love, hope, ambition, or control) or imagined. Threatened loss, according to grief recovery counselors, is the most difficult to handle.[17] The phone conversation with my friend is an example of threatened loss, something not here yet but straining a relationship that needed profound intimacy.

Norman Wright tells us that "if you don't recognize something as a loss, then you don't spend time and energy dealing with it and grieving over it, and it's captured inside you just waiting for the next loss to occur. Then it really impacts you."[18] Multiple losses extend our grieving. "Old losses actually contaminate, intensify, and complicate . . . new loss."[19] In reality, Jacob experienced multiple losses in his life that the force of Rachel's death only compounded. They included the rape of his daughter Dinah, the death of his mother, Rebekah (whom he never had the chance to say goodbye to), and then the death of his mother's maidservant. In addition, we must consider his loss of face when he lied to his father and usurped the birthright from Esau. Jacob also experienced loss when his father Isaac died and when Joseph disappeared. Furthermore, he lost his home when Esau threatened his life, and finally his strength and ability to walk when the angel touched his hip. Talk about wrestling! Jacob had an overflowing cup of losses.

Grief is the intense emotional pain that accompanies loss. When we grieve, we express three things: our feelings, our protests toward the situation, and the effects of the loss on our life.[20] Though it's a natural part of life, everyone experiences grief differently. It often lasts longer and is harder than expected. No matter how disruptive, it is a journey that cannot be rushed. To be healthy, we cannot remain in grief but must go forward. "We recover from loss by learning to grieve."[21] "Grief is the manner or process in which we work through this loss."[22]

Such "grief is not an enemy or a sign of weakness. It is a sign of being human. It is the cost of loving someone."[23] We grieve because we care and are willing to bring our total attention to the fact of loss. Because life and the things we have lost matter, we grieve. Grief notices and attends, savors and delights in life's details and relationships. Loss entered into, accepted, and owned can be healing. It is no less painful, but it is no longer debilitating.[24]

HOPE FOR THE HURTING

"The depression into which [Jacob] had fallen with the loss of Rachel became a consuming longing for death."[25] After Joseph vanishes and he presumes him dead, the patriarch wants to die. When he learns that Joseph lives in Egypt, his response is "I will go and see him before I die" (Gen. 45:28). "Even when he descended into [Egypt] and beheld with his own eyes the magnificence of Egypt's viceroy and the life of ease and comfort that awaited him as an aged, honored father, his mind dwelt upon the single thought that had followed him from the time of Rachel's death."[26] "Now let me die," he says to Joseph, "since I have seen your face, that you are still alive" (Gen. 46:30, NASB). "Jacob's mourning was the last of the trials of love, and

Jacob's lamentation was the darkest proof of Rachel's compelling presence beyond the grave."[27]

Jacob lived with Rachel's memory till the end, grieving to his very last breath. At the news that Jacob was dying, Joseph brought his two sons to his father's bed for a final blessing. The patriarch sat up and recounted the past, telling Rachel's son that God had appeared to him in Canaan and blessed him with the blessing of the land and the blessing of children. Then he said a surprising thing to Joseph: "Now I am adopting as my own sons these two boys of yours, Ephraim and Manasseh, who were born here in the land of Egypt before I arrived. They will inherit from me just as Reuben and Simeon will. But the children born to you in the future will be your own" (Gen. 48:5, 6, NLT). In effect, Jacob raised the status of Joseph's two sons to that of tribal heads. The grandsons of Rachel would thus inherit the land as equals with the sons of Leah and the handmaids. Jacob thus enlarged Rachel's heirs from two to four, giving her what she had dreamed of all her life.[28] It was his parting gift to her memory. Furthermore, he blessed his grandsons that day: "The people of Israel will use your names to bless each other. They will say, 'May God make you as prosperous as Ephraim and Manasseh'" (verse 20, NLT). Thus he vindicated Rachel, increased her sons, and saw the nation of Israel's blessings flow through her children. And Joseph? He received a double portion, the birthright (verses 21, 22, 29).[29]

During that extraordinary moment of surprise blessing, Jacob fixed his mind on Rachel herself and wandered into a last reverie. Drifting far off as in a daydream, he recalled their relationship—his undying love for her, their marriage, the two sons she bore, and her tragic death. "When I came from Paddan, Rachel died, to my sorrow, in the land of Canaan on the journey, when there was still some distance to go to Ephrath; and I buried her there on the way to Ephrath (that is, Bethlehem)" (verse 7, NASB). The patriarch still missed Rachel after all those years. His suffering from her death continued. As his thoughts wandered far away from Egypt and Joseph, into the most private world of memory and sorrow, longing, and loneliness, for a moment he was with his beloved Rachel. Then, recovering from this reverie he looked at the two sons of Joseph, whom he had just adopted as his own and who were surely familiar to him and for a second he did not recognize them. In that intense instant of yearning to be with Rachel, weak and dim of sight, he failed to make out his own grandsons. "Who are these?" he asks Joseph (verse 8, NASB).

One of the myths of loss is that "time heals all wounds." "Give it time, it'll be OK." "Time will take care of it." But it's not true. Loss is with us forever. To erase it is to deny our history, and to diminish it is to lessen the one we love. When my friend died, her husband told me, "Pastor, it hurts. Bad! I'm so lonely. They tell me I'll get over it," he went after a long sigh, "but I don't want to get over it." It wasn't the pain he wanted to cling to—it was Ileene. She would be with him forever. That's authentic grief.

A grieving parent attached the following poem in memory of Sonja Lynn "Stroud" Sanders to the chain-link Memorial Fence at the Murrah Memorial. It included pictures of Sonja as well as her two daughters whom she'd left behind:

"Go ahead and mention my child,
    the one that got killed, you know.
Don't worry about hurting me further;
    the depth of my pain doesn't show.
Don't worry about making me cry.
    I'm already crying inside.
Help me to heal by releasing
    the tears that I cry and hide.
I'm hurt when you just keep silent,
    pretending she didn't exist.
I'd rather you mention my child,
    knowing at least she'd been missed.
You asked me how I was doing.
    I say "Pretty good" or "Fine."
But healing is something ongoing;
    I feel it will take a lifetime."

"I feel it will take a lifetime." It will. That's what I told Maggie in my pastor's class when she described how many kept telling her she would get over her loss. "No, you won't," I said.

In sharing his journey of grief after the loss of his beloved Joy, C. S. Lewis wrote that the one thing he had learned from her extended illness and untimely death was that the price of love is grief.[30] Grief comes with loss because we love. We hurt because we love. Because love goes on, hurt will linger. The deeper the love, the more intense the loss. But the alternative—no intimacy—is unacceptable. The only way to stop hurting is to seal oneself off from meaningful relationships. Thus to love is to risk the hurt of loss. Authentic intimacy would have it no other way.

But is there hope for the hurting? Did Jacob go down to the grave in unresolved grief? Is that to be everyone's lot? No! During the 17 years Jacob lived in Egypt his grief found balance and hope. While it did not go away, it did become healthier, transforming into "good grief." His reverie of Rachel at the end of his life was not the kind of immobilizing grief that he had experienced earlier. His grief lost the kind of dysfunction that had brought so much pain to others around him. Promise finally filled Jacob's grief. It could hope. While he was still sad and lonely, still longing to hear her voice and feel her embrace, his way of dealing with it was different. It was healthy and reconciled. God had given him 17 years of life in Egypt during which he lived in grand style, surrounded by his large family of children and grandchildren. They provided for his every need. In the blessings of those years free of further loss and trial his heart opened once again to hope.

The watershed came with the reappearance of Joseph. It was like a dream come true. His son's emergence after so many years opened a window of hope in Jacob's shattered soul. God's doing and a miracle, it gave him promise of final resolution. When he looked on the face of his restored son and experienced the tranquillity of life in Egypt with Rachel's son, Jacob knew that God's promises would not fail. As Dresner writes: "Marked for death himself, Joseph rises from the pit to bring life to those around him: to the nations whom he delivers from the dread famine that devastated the ancient Middle

East for seven years, to his mourning father who lives in honor in Egypt for seventeen years, and to the brothers who thought to send him to his grave."[31] The reappearance of Joseph brings life to those around him. Because of him, his father and others experience contentment and security. Grief was still there, but it was good grief! In that peace and hope Jacob could pass on blessings to each one of his sons. He could bring the family together, finally, after so many years of dysfunction and brokenness (Gen. 49:1-28). And he could hold out hope for God's final visit (Gen. 48:21) when Jacob could once again embrace Rachel.

Jacob's loss of Rachel and his resulting grief became a watershed that changed his life forever. His grief was lonely. Encompassed and compounded by multiple losses, it created unhealthy choices and dysfunctional behaviors that embroiled his family in turmoil for decades. In fact, it extended throughout the rest of his life and was on his heart the moment he died. Through it all, though, God opened a window of hope that Jacob chose to look through, believe, and embrace. There he found healing, comfort, hope, expectation—and peace!

Is there hope for the hurting? Yes. We find it in the windows of hope that God opens to us through what He has done, is doing, and promises to do for us.

"My soul weeps with grief," David declared, "encourage me by Your Word" (Ps. 119:28, paraphrase).

Ultimately, grief recovery has to do with words—God's words. What He has to say about our loss and His promise and plan and power to help us both now and in the future. Listen to just two of His promises for weary loss-filled hearts.

"Blessed *be* the God and Father of our Lord Jesus Christ," Paul writes, "the Father of mercies and God of all comfort, who comforts us in all our affliction so that we will be able to comfort those who are in any affliction with the comfort with which we ourselves are comforted by God. For just as the sufferings of Christ are ours in abundance, so also our comfort is abundant through Christ" (2 Cor. 1:3-5, NASB).

"And now, brothers and sisters, I want you to know what will happen to the Christians who have died so you will not be full of sorrow like people who have no hope. For since we believe that Jesus died and was raised to life again, we also believe that when Jesus comes, God will bring back with Jesus all the Christians who have died. I can tell you this directly from the Lord: We who are still living when the Lord returns will not rise to meet him ahead of those who are in their graves. For the Lord himself will come down from heaven with a commanding shout, with the call of the archangel, and with the trumpet call of God. First, all the Christians who have died will rise from their graves. Then, together with them, we who are still alive and remain on the earth will be caught up in the clouds to meet the Lord in the air and remain with him forever. So comfort and encourage each other with these words" (1 Thess. 4:13-18, NLT).

God never told us not to grieve. He only asks that we don't grieve like those who have no hope. When our soul weeps with grief, it is His Word that soothes, bringing peace, hope, and courage. Only the grip of Jacob's God gives us hope when we wrestle with the enemy called death.

---

[1] Roger Rosenblatt, "How We Remember," *Time,* May 29, 2000, pp. 26-28.
[2] *Ibid.,* p. 30.
[3] *Ibid.,* p. 28.
[4] S. Dresner, *Rachel,* p. 184.
[5] *Ibid.,* pp. 175-205. Palestinian rioters have attacked it as a symbol of Jewish presence in their territory.
[6] *Ibid.,* p. 100.
[7] *Ibid.,* p. 102.
[8] *Ibid.,* p. 101.
[9] N. Rosenblatt and J. Horwitz, *Wrestling With Angels,* p. 378.
[10] Dresner, pp. 102, 103.
[11] Naomi Rosenblatt and Joshua Horwitz, p. 319.
[12] Dresner, p. 178.
[13] Rosenblatt and Horwitz, p. 319.
[14] Dresner, p. 110.
[15] *GriefShare* (Wake Forest, N.C.: Church Initiative, Inc., 1999), p. 19.
[16] See H. Norman Wright, *Crisis Care: Hope for the Hurting* (Richardson, Tex.: Grace Products Corporation, 1996), p. 97.
[17] *Ibid.,* p. 86.
[18] *Ibid.*
[19] *GriefShare,* p. 26.
[20] Wright, p. 98.
[21] *Ibid.,* p. 88.

[22] *GriefShare,* p. 29.

[23] *Ibid.*

[24] Eugene H. Peterson, *Leap Over a Wall* (San Francisco: Harper San Francisco, 1997), pp. 115, 119, 121.

[25] Dresner, p. 110.

[26] *Ibid.*

[27] *Ibid.*

[28] *Ibid.,* p. 139.

[29] Ellen White notes that "these youths were connected, through their mother, with the highest order of the Egyptian priesthood; and the position of their father opened to them the avenues to wealth and distinction, should they choose to connect themselves with the Egyptians. It was Joseph's desire, however, that they should unite with their own people. He manifested his faith in the covenant promise, in behalf of his sons renouncing all the honors that the court of Egypt offered, for a place among the despised shepherd tribes, to whom had been entrusted the oracles of God" *(Patriarchs and Prophets,* p. 234).

[30] See Brian Sibley, *C. S. Lewis Through the Shadowlands: The Story of His Life With Joy Davidman* (Grand Rapids: Fleming H. Revel, 1999).

[31] Dresner, p. 111.

BURY ME NOT

twelve

(Genesis 47:27-31 — 50:1-14)

During a college pilgrimage to mobster Al Capone's burial site, "Jim Tipton wondered whether he could duplicate on the Web the 'paparazzi thrill' he experienced in that 'presence of fame.' In February 1996 Tipton launched Find a Grave, a searchable online database that quickly grew to include more than 10,000 listings of the late and great, from historical personalities to movie stars. Most entries featured birth and death dates, information on burial locations, even photos of the tombstones." In just four years the Salt Lake City Web designer-cum-digital graveyard caretaker had succeeded beyond his wildest dreams. Find a Grave was pulling in an average of 20,000 people daily. Just click on www.findagrave.com.

"It was the summation of life in one small patch of ground—rather than any ghoulish appeal—that has fueled his interest in burial sites. 'The [graves] that usually move me are the simple ones,' Tipton says. *I Love Lucy* star Lucille Ball's final resting place—marked by a small plaque tucked away in a Forest Lawn mausoleum in Los Angeles—never fails to put it all in perspective for him. 'She was cremated and put in a little niche in a wall,' Tipton says. 'It's this huge wall, and [the many burial plaques] all become a blur when you step back. This person was a huge name in life, and it's just her name on a stone amongst others' now.'"[1]

More than half the final chapter of Genesis describes the mourning and burial of Jacob (Gen. 50:1-14). Joseph mourned, throwing himself on his father, weeping over him, and kissing him (verse 1).

And the Egyptians mourned (verse 3). Both Joseph and the Egyptians made great preparations for Jacob's burial. The prime minister told his morticians to embalm his father's body. The embalming process took 40 days, and the nation mourned for 70 days (verse 3). When the period of mourning ended, Pharaoh granted Joseph's special request to bury Jacob in his homeland. "So Joseph went, with a great number of Pharaoh's counselors and advisers—all the senior officers of Egypt. Joseph also took his brothers and the entire household of Jacob. . . . So a great number of chariots, cavalry, and people accompanied Joseph. When they arrived at the threshing floor of Atad, near the Jordan River, they held a very great and solemn funeral, with a seven-day period of mourning for Joseph's father. The local residents, the Canaanites, renamed the place Abel-mizraim, for they said, 'This is a place of very deep mourning for these Egyptians.' So Jacob's sons did as he had commanded them. They carried his body to the land of Canaan and buried it there in the cave of Machpelah. This is the cave that Abraham had bought for a permanent burial place in the field of Ephron the Hittite, near Mamre" (verses 7-13, NLT). Thus "Jacob, who fought his way into life, departs life just as dramatically."[2]

The writer of Genesis "seems to go out of his way to emphasize in detail the magnitude of the mourning" over Jacob.[3] As Sailhamer notes: "The question naturally arises why the text gives such detail on the burial of Jacob when the accounts of the death of the other patriarchs give only the bare facts that they died and were buried. Even the account of Joseph's death, which is also recorded in this chapter, consists only of the brief notice that he died and was embalmed and entombed in Egypt. Was his burial of any less magnitude than Jacob's? Surely it was not, but the narrative devotes virtually no attention to it. Why then the emphasis on Jacob's burial?"[4]

Could it be that Genesis too has an interest in burial sites? That the summation of life in one small patch of ground—in this case a cave—is significant? That Jacob's name is not just a mere name on a stone among others, somehow lost in the blur of other notables (or nobodies) buried in that distant cave called Machpelah?

What do Jacob's final days and burial site say about our existential wrestlings? about family and God? Summing life up in one small patch of ground can be evocative, especially when you grasp what that life was all about and what that patch of ground may signify.

I believe the focus is on God's faithfulness to His promises to families and the hope they have in the eventual realization of those promised blessings. We also touch the person of Jacob. For it is often the later years that reveal one's true self and express one's true values. Additionally, during both the funeral procession that extended more than 200 miles and his burial, the Egyptians and the Canaanites witnessed what God had done and could do. Certainly everyone knew why Jacob was being buried where he was. It was an opportunity for his sons to tell his story and about his God.

Nor was Jacob's name to be lost in the blur of names etched upon human history. The Lord is the God of Abraham, Isaac, and Jacob (Ex. 3:6; Isa. 41:8; Matt. 8:11; 22:32; Luke 20:37). Surprisingly, God condescends to assume the incongruous title "the God of Jacob" (Ps. 20:1). We would expect "the God of Abraham, father of the faithful," or "the God of Moses, friend of God." But the God of Jacob, the swindler? Surely not! Yet, "Jacob have I loved," God announces (Mal. 1:2, 3; Rom. 9:13; Ps. 47:4). "'Do not be afraid, O worm Jacob, . . . for I myself will help you,' declares the Lord, your Redeemer, the Holy One of Israel" (Isa. 41:14, NIV). "He stoops to associate Himself on terms of intimacy with one of the weakest and least attractive of our race. What is weaker or more worthless than a worm? And yet that 'worm,' subject of the relentless, pursuing love of God, becomes a prince, having power with God and men."[5] Surely, there is hope for every one of us. For every family on earth. "The Lord of hosts *is* with us; the God of Jacob *is* our refuge," the psalmist writes (Ps. 46:11, NKJV). "For the Lord Most High *is* awesome; *He is* a great King over all the earth. . . . He will choose our inheritance for us, the excellence of Jacob whom He loves" (Ps. 47:2-4, NKJV). The name Jacob looms large in Scripture.

GOLDEN YEARS

When the way opened for Jacob to take his family to Egypt to meet Joseph, he wondered about God's approval. "Can I really go down to Egypt? Can I truly go there for Joseph's sake? My grandfather Abraham sinned while in Egypt. God reproached him, and he returned. Isaac wanted to go to Egypt when he met famine, but God warned him not to. If I go down to Egypt, what will happen to God's promises? What will become of this land, God's inheritance?" So Jacob stopped at Beersheba and offered sacrifices (Gen. 46:1). He wanted to know God's will. His concern about whether or not he should visit Egypt to see Joseph shows how much he had grown in faith. Jacob waited until God revealed Himself again, indicating that the patriarch was a different person than whom he had been years before.

"And God spoke to Israel in a vision at night and said, 'Jacob! Jacob!' 'Here I am,' he replied. 'I am God, the God of your father,' he said. 'Do not be afraid to go down to Egypt, for I will make you into a great nation there. I will go down to Egypt with you, and I will surely bring you back again. And Joseph's own hand will close your eyes'" (verses 2-4, NIV). It was a fourfold promise to Jacob: God would make him a great nation while in Egypt; he would not be alone, because God's gracious presence would accompany him into Egypt; God would surely bring him back to the land promised to him and his family; and though he would die in Egypt, his son Joseph would be at his side till the end. With these promises ringing in his ears, Jacob left Beersheba for Egypt, taking with him "his sons and grandsons and his daughters and granddaughters—all his offspring" (verse 5, NIV), along with their livestock and the possessions they had acquired in Canaan.

When Jacob's entourage arrived in Egypt, officials directed them to Goshen where Joseph had arranged for them to settle. It was here that Joseph came up to meet his father for the first time in years. Rachel's son arrived in his state chariot, attended by a princely retinue. It was an emotional moment. Forgetting the splendor of his surroundings and the dignity of his position, Joseph sprang from this chariot and ran ahead to embrace his father, throwing his arms around him and weeping on his shoulder for a long long time (verse 29).[6] "I can die now, having seen for myself that you are still alive,"

Jacob finally says (verse 30, NRSV). But Jacob didn't die. "Seventeen years were yet to be granted him in the peaceful retirement of Goshen. These years were in happy contrast to those that had preceded them. He saw in his sons evidence of true repentance; he saw his family surrounded by all the conditions needful for the development of a great nation; and his faith grasped the sure promise of their future establishment in Canaan. He himself was surrounded with every token of love and favor that the prime minister of Egypt could bestow; and happy in the society of his long-lost son, he passed down gently and peacefully to the grave."[7]

THE BLESSING

When the end for Jacob came, he summoned all of his sons together in order to bless them and to foretell the future of their lives and of the tribes that would descend from them (Gen. 49:1-28). Three things concerned him: making sure the nation of Israel's blessing would flow through the children of Rachel (Gen. 48:8-22);[8] blessing each son and unfolding the future of their families (Gen. 49:2-28); and arranging for his burial in the family cave of Machpelah back in Canaan (Gen. 47:29-31; 49:29-33). It was a fitting climax that demonstrated the power of God's prevailing grace in his life and for his family.

One by one Jacob blessed his children. In the process "the power of God rested upon him, and under the influence of Inspiration he was constrained to declare the truth, however painful."[9] "Before him in prophetic vision the future of his descendants was unfolded. One after another the names of his sons were mentioned, the character of each was described, and the future history of the tribe was briefly foretold."[10] He noted their achievements and their shortcomings, their past deeds and their prospects for the future. "Each received a blessing that was appropriate to him" (Gen. 49:28, NLT).

The book of Hebrews tells us that these moments of final blessing were an act of faith and worship: "By faith Jacob, as he was dying, blessed each of the sons of Joseph, and worshiped, leaning on the top of his staff" (Heb. 11:21, NASB). The patriarch was consciously passing on a legacy of faith, hope, and meaning, writing (renewing) as it were his family mission statement on his deathbed. How many sons and daughters have left a parent's death wondering where they were with God? How many spouses or parents or siblings have gone away from their loved one's death with similar angst? As Naomi Rosenblatt and Joshua Horwitz write: "The most enduring legacy we can bequeath to our children is a clear articulation of who we are and what we stand for. We can leave them financial assets, but those can lose their value. A family business can go bankrupt. A family home can burn down. But if we can make clear to our children who we are, where we have come from, and what we value, then they can begin to build their own personal identity based on a solid foundation."[11] We cannot assume that our children (or other family members) will absorb our values through osmosis. Like Jacob, we need to spell them out explicitly.

Covey notes that "in the end, life teaches us what is important, and that is family. Often for people on their deathbed, things not done in the family are a source of greatest regret. And hospice volunteers report that in many cases unresolved issues—particularly with family members—seem to keep people holding on, clinging to life until there is a resolution—an acknowledging, an apologizing, a forgiving—that brings peace and release."[12] Some of the greatest pain comes when such interpersonal and family closure has not taken place. Fortunately, Jacob had been careful to bring such closure. He had forgiven his sons, loved them to the last, blessed them, given them a legacy of faith, hope, and meaning—saying those ever so important things before he died.[13] "Family is one of the few permanent roles in life, perhaps the only truly permanent role."[14] What we do and say to each other in life and at death forever imprints our sense of self. Jacob's blessing would continue to linger in the moral-spiritual imagination of his posterity.

Eugene Roop observes that "many of us live in a culture in which we do not know how to die: a world of machines and sterile hospital rooms, where the final actions are likely to be a frantic hospital alert and a hasty family gathering. The world we leave is often not the family world left by Jacob."[15] But perhaps by listening closely to accounts like his, "we can discover ways in which we can gather up our own lives and assist the next generation as they step into God's future."[16]

BURY ME NOT

Though his family had prospered in Egypt, Jacob reminded his sons that their sojourn in the land was only temporary. The land of promise was their home. He made them swear to return his body to that land of promise so the next generation wouldn't forget where they had come from and where they were destined to return. "'Soon I will die. Bury me with my father and grandfather in the cave in Ephron's field. This is the cave in the field of Machpelah, near Mamre in Canaan, which Abraham bought from Ephron the Hittite for a permanent burial place. There Abraham and his wife Sarah are buried. There Isaac and his wife, Rebekah, are buried. And there I buried Leah. It is the cave that my grandfather Abraham bought from the Hittites.' Then when Jacob had finished this charge to his sons, he lay back in the bed, breathed his last, and died" (Gen. 49:29-33, NLT).

Summing life up in one small patch of ground can be evocative, especially when you grasp what that life was all about and what that patch of ground may signify. As Roop again notes, "The desire to be buried with one's ancestors was central to the Hebrew approach of death. Generally this involved burial in a family tomb or property. And yet the need to be buried with the ancestors touched a need that ran deeper than the geographical location of the burial. Burial was invested with the hope that not even death could break the family bond. . . . To be buried with the ancestors helped solidify that bond."[17] For Jacob, that family bond reached beyond mere human aspirations of solidarity, personal identity, and remembrance. It encompassed the incredible promise and purpose of God. Jacob's family glue embodied God's moral spiritual horizon and his family's unique place among the families of the earth: "All the families of the earth will be blessed through you and your descendants" (Gen. 28:14, NLT; 35:9-12; 12:1-3). "I am about to die," Jacob had told

Joseph earlier, "but God will be with you and will bring you again to Canaan, the land of your ancestors" (Gen. 48:21, NLT). The patriarch wanted to be buried in the Land of Promise so that he could be resurrected from it. He wanted to rest in the Land of Promise so that his family would have an ongoing witness of his hope. Jacob had an active faith that enabled him to believe God.

Yes, Genesis has an interest in burial sites. The summation of life in one small patch of ground—in this case a cave—is significant for every believer. Jacob grounded his burial request in the promise of land that God had given to his family through Abraham. His death forces our attention beyond even the Exodus to Israel's nationhood and the coming of the Messiah. It directs us down to the very end of time with the return of Jesus Christ, the resurrection of the dead, and the final return of God's people to the Land of Promise—the earth made new, Eden restored. At last the long-sought blessing will be realized for believing families.

Jacob's final days and burial site says much about our existential wrestlings. It points to God's faithfulness to His promises to families and the hope they have in the eventual realization of those promised blessings. God will be with you and will bring you again to the Promised Land. Jacob's last words are words of hope in God's power. He envisions the day when, through the Lord's gracious blessing and almighty power, he will be alive again—bodily—and taste that promised blessing for himself. In the end, Jacob's hope rests squarely on faith in the power of the living God.

WORSHIP

Scripture tells us that "by faith Jacob, as he was dying, . . . worshiped, leaning on the top of his staff" (Heb. 11:21, NASB; see Gen. 47:31). The life of Jacob, which stretches over half the book of Genesis (including the Joseph narratives), has seen his family through moments of trust and betrayal, sterility and fertility, feast and famine, separation and reunion, wrestling and peace, all within the promise and providence of God. "Jacob had sinned, and had deeply suffered. Many years of toil, care, and sorrow had been his since the day when his great sin caused him to flee from his father's tents. A homeless fugitive, separated from his mother, whom he never saw again; laboring seven years for her whom he loved, only to be basely cheated; toiling twenty years in the service of a covetous and grasping kinsman; seeing his wealth increasing, and sons rising around him, but finding little joy in the contentious and divided household; distressed by his daughter's shame, by her brothers' revenge, by the death of Rachel, by the unnatural crime of Reuben, by Judah's sin, by the cruel deception and malice practiced toward Joseph—how long and dark is the catalogue of evils spread out to view! Again and again he had reaped the fruit of that first wrong deed. Over and over he saw repeated among his sons the sins of which he himself had been guilty."[18] Talk about wrestling!

Now, his "last years brought an evening of tranquility and repose after a troubled and weary day. Clouds had gathered dark above his path, yet his sun set clear, and the radiance of heaven illumined his parting hours."[19] Jacob had come to learn firsthand that God "does not treat us as our sins deserve or repay us according to our iniquities. For as high as the heavens are above the earth, so great is his love for those who fear him; as far as the east is from the west, so far has he removed our transgressions from us. As a father has compassion on his children, so the Lord has compassion on those who fear him; for he knows how we are formed, he remembers that we are dust" (Ps. 103:10-14, NIV). His family was together, his beloved Joseph alive. God's promises for his family rang loudly in his ears. He could envision the day when he would embrace Rachel again. No wonder he would be grateful—and worship the God who had made it all possible.

No! Jacob's name is not just a mere name on a stone among many, somehow lost in the blur of other notables (or nobodies) buried in that distant cave called Machpelah. His name will forever be linked with those who pour out their soul in grateful adoration to the God who keeps His promises and will remember their families.

---

[1] A. S. Berman, "A Grave New World Online: The Famous and the Not-So-Famous Get Eternal Home," *USA Today,* June 29, 2000.

[2] E. Roop, *Genesis,* p. 290.

[3] J. Sailhamer, *The Pentateuch as Narrative,* p. 238.

[4] *Ibid.,* p. 238; see also Roop, p. 290.

[5] J. O. Sanders, *Spiritual Manpower,* pp. 29, 30.

[6] E. G. White, *Patriarchs and Prophets,* p. 233.

[7] *Ibid.,* p. 233.

[8] As noted earlier, Jacob lived with Rachel's memory till the end.

[9] White, *Patriarchs and Prophets,* p. 237.

[10] *Ibid.,* p. 235.

[11] N. Rosenblatt and J. Horwitz, *Wrestling With Angels,* p. 376.

[12] S. Covey, *The 7 Habits of Highly Effective Families,* p. 116.

[13] White, *Patriarchs and Prophets,* pp. 232, 237.

[14] Covey, p. 116.

[15] Roop, p. 295.

[16] *Ibid.*

[17] *Ibid.,* p. 289.

[18] White, *Patriarchs and Prophets,* pp. 237, 238.

[19] *Ibid.,* p. 237.

EPILOGUE

TOUCHED BY AN ANGEL

Since its debut in September 1994 CBS's hit television series *Touched by an Angel* has affected millions of lives with its warmth, wisdom, and humor. It's a captivating series about angels who come to us as companions, helpers, and champions of deliverance. Tess, the gruff but goodhearted supervisor angel, steers both her trainees and their human "assignments" back on the right path. Monica, the softhearted novice angel, helps people facing crossroads in their lives who need to hear that God loves them. And Andrew, the kindly, compassionate angel of death, eases people toward life's final reality—death. Unlike other hit series, the show attracts a group of viewers who are looking for more than entertainment and who feel that its warm cast of characters and the wisdom conveyed in its dialogues genuinely "touch" their hearts and influence their lives. Already a book, *When Angels Speak,* has culled a collection of quotations from its scripts. Now the words of Monica, Tess, and Andrew can be with you every day, everywhere.

The popularity of the program is part of a rising grassroots fascination with angels. What idea could be more beguiling than the notion of beings, free of the limitations of time, space, and human weakness, hovering between us and all harm? In the past decade angels have lodged deep in the popular imagination. We find angels-only boutiques, angel newsletters, angel seminars, and angel Web sites. A *Time* magazine poll indicates that most Americans now believe in angels. Harvard Divinity School has a course on angels, and Boston College has two. Bookstores have had to establish angel sections as books about angels continue to be on the religious best-seller list. "These are desperate times," says Peter Kreeft, a philosophy professor at Boston College. "People seek supernatural solutions to their problems. We want to reassure ourselves of our spirtualism."[1] In a secular world driven by scientific method, "angels are the reassurance that the supernatural and the realm of God are real,"[2] says Richard Woods, a Dominican priest and an author of books on angels and demons. Where disaster confronts us on all sides and the moral spiritual issues of our postmodern world are so confusing, people search for simple answers.

Angels loom large in the story of Jacob. They fill the patriarch's imagination and sense of reality. Angels are his companions, helpers, champions of deliverance, comforters, even antagonists. They dominate his dream at Bethel when he flees from his brother. "As he slept, he dreamed of a stairway that reached from earth to heaven. And he saw the angels of God going up and down on it. At the top of the stairway stood the Lord, and he said, 'I am the Lord, the God of your grandfather Abraham and the God of your father, Isaac. The ground you are lying on belongs to you. I will give it to you and your descendants. Your descendants will be as numerous as the dust of the earth! They will cover the land from east to west and from north to south. All the families of the earth will be blessed through you and your descendants. What's more, I will be with you, and I will protect you wherever you go. I will someday bring you safely back to this land. I will be with you constantly until I have finished giving you everything I have promised.' Then Jacob woke up and said, 'Surely the Lord is in this place, and I wasn't even aware of it.' He was afraid and said, 'What an awesome place this is! It is none other than the house of God—the gateway to heaven!'" (Gen. 28:12-17, NLT).

Jacob told his wives that an angel of God gave him the idea of selective breeding that finally enabled him to become financially successful and escape Laban's grasping hand (Gen. 31:11-13). Interestingly, during his anxiety-filled journey homeward to Esau and his father, Isaac, Jacob encountered two bands of angels. "As Jacob and his household started on their way again, angels of God came to meet him. When Jacob saw them, he exclaimed, 'This is God's camp!' So he named the place Mahanaim" (Gen. 32:1, 2, NLT). The name Mahanaim means "two camps." Jacob noted two camps of travelers—

his family and the angels. God was camping where his family did, thus accompanying them. The Lord was granting him a token of divine care by allowing him to see the angels. "As he traveled southward from Mount Gilead, two hosts of heavenly angels seemed to encompass him behind and before, advancing with his company, as if for their protection. Jacob remembered the vision at Bethel so long before, and his burdened heart grew lighter at this evidence that the divine messengers who had brought him hope and courage at his flight from Canaan were to be the guardians of his return."[3]

And yet even though attended by angels, Jacob felt that he had something to do to secure his own safety. So he divided his people and cattle into "two camps" (verse 7). The phrase "two camps" in this verse is the same Hebrew as the name Mahanaim in the previous passage. "Jacob divided his people and cattle into *Mahanaim*. He used this *Mahanaim* to replace that other *Mahanaim*. Originally, Jacob had one band on earth and God had one band in heaven, but now Jacob divided his band into two."[4] The goal of Jacob's scheme was to provide a way of escape. Evidently, he did not consider the angels sufficient protection in his pending confrontation with Esau.

So Jacob finds himself not only surrounded by angels, but wrestling all night long with *the* Angel (verses 22-30). As Hosea writes: "Before Jacob was born, he struggled with his brother; when he became a man, he even fought with God. Yes, he wrestled with the angel and won. He wept and pleaded for a blessing from him. There at Bethel he met God face to face, and God spoke to him— the Lord God Almighty, the Lord is his name!" (Hosea 12:3-5, NLT).

Ellen White notes that during the closing moments of blessing with his sons, "God by the spirit of prophecy elevated the mind of Jacob above his natural feelings. In his last hours angels were all around him, and the power of the grace of God shone upon him. His paternal feelings would have led him to only utter in his dying testimony expressions of love and tenderness. But under the influence of inspiration he uttered truth, although painful."[5] Jacob was obviously conscious of the heavenly messengers when he said, "Gather around me, and I will tell you what is going to happen to you in the days to come" (Gen. 49:1, NLT). "Often and anxiously he had thought of their future, and had endeavored to picture to himself the history of the different tribes. Now as his children waited to receive his last blessing the Spirit of Inspiration rested upon him, and before him in prophetic vision the future of his descendants was unfolded."[6] Angels have always played an active role in the spirit of inspiration (Rev. 19:10; 22:9; 21:9; 17:1; Dan. 8:16, 17; 9:20-22), and it was something that Jacob had come to know personally.

Jacob, while reviewing his life history, recognized the sustaining power of God when he blessed Joseph's sons. "May the God before whom my fathers Abraham and Isaac walked, the God who has been my shepherd all my life to this day, the Angel who has delivered me from all harm—may he bless these boys. May they be called by my name and the names of my fathers Abraham and Isaac, and may they increase greatly upon the earth" (Gen. 48:15, 16, NIV). "The Angel who has delivered me from all harm"—that's how Jacob saw it. Wherever and whenever angels were at work for him and his family, God was at hand. Jacob knew from personal experience what Paul later wrote about being touched by an angel: "In speaking of the angels he says, 'He makes his angels winds, his servants flames of fire.' . . . To which of the angels did God ever say, 'Sit at my right hand until I make your enemies a footstool for your feet'? Are not all angels ministering spirits sent to serve those who will inherit salvation?" (Heb. 1:7-14, NIV). "For He will give His angels charge concerning you, to guard you in all your ways" (Ps. 91:11, NASB). And it is the angel of the Lord who "encamps all around those who fear Him, and delivers them" (Ps. 34:7, NKJV).

As with Jacob, God promises the ministry of angels to every one of us and our families. We may not dream about them, see them, or physically wrestle with them as Jacob did. Nevertheless, they are there, behind the scenes of our lives, involved in all our existential wrestlings as individuals and family. Sometimes, as did Jacob, we unwittingly wrestle with them as they minister in our behalf, whether by way of protection or prompting us to do what is right. Ultimately, such wrestling with angels—whether metaphoric for all

our human struggling with life's family-oriented existential questions as proposed in this book or real-to-life as in Jacob's experience—comes down to our wrestling with God. Behind all our existential wrestlings in family stands God and His ministering spirits,
the angels.

Hosea tells us that Jacob "fought with God. Yes, he wrestled with
the angel and won. He wept and pleaded for a blessing from him"
(Hosea 12:3, 4, NLT). Jacob beat God. He beat the Angel (and
angels). And he won! His victory, though, came through weeping
and in pleading for a blessing (wrestling). "I will not let you go until
you bless me!" he cried. In that momentous surrender, God *threw*
Jacob. And Jacob won. The patriarch took the long-sought blessing
because God took the heart.

So it will ever be, whether personally or in the family. The long-
sought blessing for self or for our family comes only when the Angel
takes the heart(s). Only when we allow God to do His work of grace
in our hearts and permit His ministering spirits to transform our
lives as well. Then and only then will our existential wrestlings cease.

Thus Jacob's story leaves us with a twofold legacy for God's end-
time people (and their families): the promise of angel ministry, and
the call to truly wrestle with God until we have been emptied of self
and receive *the blessing*. Jacob's history is "an assurance that God will
not cast off those who have been deceived and tempted and betrayed
into sin, but who have returned unto Him with true repentance.
While Satan seeks to destroy this class, *God will send His angels to comfort and protect them in the time of peril*. The assaults of Satan are fierce
and determined, his delusions are terrible; but the Lord's eye is upon
His people, and His ear listens to their cries. Their affliction is great,
the flames of the furnace seem about to consume them; but the
Refiner will bring them forth as gold tried in the fire. God's love for
His children during the period of their severest trial is as strong and
tender as in the days of their sunniest prosperity; but it is needful for
them to be placed in the furnace of fire; their earthliness must be consumed, that the image of Christ may be perfectly reflected.

"The season of distress and anguish before us will require a faith that can endure weariness, delay, and hunger—a faith that will not faint though severely tried. The period of probation is granted to all to prepare for that time. Jacob prevailed because he was persevering and determined. His victory is an evidence of the power of importunate prayer. All who will lay hold of God's promises, as he did, and be as earnest and persevering as he was, will succeed as he succeeded. Those who are unwilling to deny self, to agonize before God, to pray long and earnestly for His blessing, will not obtain it. *Wrestling with God—how few know what it is!* How few have ever had their souls drawn out after God with intensity of desire until every power is on the stretch. When waves of despair which no language can express sweep over the suppliant, how few cling with unyielding faith to the promises of God."[7]

---

[1] Nancy Gibbs, "Angels Among Us," *Time,* Dec. 27, 1993, pp. 58, 59.

[2] *Ibid.,* p. 62.

[3] E. G. White, *Patriarchs and Prophets,* p. 195.

[4] W. Nee, *The God of Abraham, Isaac & Jacob,* p. 129.

[5] Ellen G. White, *Spiritual Gifts* (Washington, D.C.: Review and Herald Pub. Assn., 1945), vol. 3, pp. 172, 173.

[6] ———— , *Patriarchs and Prophets,* p. 235.

[7] ———— , *The Great Controversy,* p. 621. (Italics supplied.)